MARGHERITA MARCHIONE

SHEPHERD OF SOULS

A PICTORIAL LIFE OF POPE PIUS XII

PAULIST PRESS
New York/Mahwah, N.J.

Photographic references:
Pontifical Museum and Gallery Monuments, Vatican City; *La Domenica del Corriere*;
La Domenica degli Italiani; *La Tribuna Illustrata*; *L'Osservatore Romano* Servizio
fotografico e foto Felici; *Annuario Pontificio*; United States Holocaust Memorial
Museum, Washington, DC; Archives: Archdiocese of Baltimore and St. Paul-
Minneapolis, Diocese of Trenton, NJ, Knights of Columbus; Religious Teachers Filippini,
Catholic University of America (Manuscripts Collection); Fordham (David Berns
Archives), Notre Dame and Seton Hall University (Special Collections).

Acknowledgments:
The author thanks Maria Fede Caproni for research assistance
and the staff of *Inside the Vatican* for help in the preparation of the manuscript.
She is grateful to Ralph M. Cestone for the financial assistance given for this publication.

"Theologian, canonist,
scholar, linguist, statesman, diplomat
all of these Pius XII was.
For all of them he has been hailed and praised.
But more than anything else
He was a pastor, a good shepherd of souls,
Selflessly dedicated to the honest interests
Of the Church and to the greater glory of God."

Richard Cardinal Cushing

First published 2002 by Libreria Editrice Vaticana – 00120 Vatican City
Copyright © 2002 by Religious Teachers Filippini, Morristown, NJ.

ISBN 0-8091-4181-7

Published in the United States of America in 2002 by
Paulist Press
997 Macarthur Boulevard
Mahwah, New Jersey, 07430

www.paulistpress.com

Printed and bound in the United States of America

To His Holiness Pope John Paul II,
who strengthened the Church in a period of turmoil,
reached out to all other religions,
and became the world's leading moral voice
for life, tolerance, charity and peace.
In this he continues and expands
the work of charity and love of Pope Pius XII—
as portrayed in photos and words in this volume.
The link between these two outstanding pontiffs
becomes more apparent the more one studies their lives.

CONTENTS

The work
of
justice
is
peace.

The Motto of
Pope Pius XII

PREFACE

Nearly half a century ago, as a seminarian beginning the study of theology, I shared in the excitement of a great rally in St. Peter's Square. More than a hundred thousand enthusiastic members of Catholic Action were there to hear and to cheer Pope Pius XII.

To this day I remember the drama of the Pope's sweeping gestures and the sense of marvel that he could deliver a long message without a text at hand. Long before the day of the teleprompter, he was able to draw upon the resources of a prodigious memory.

For many, Pope Pius XII was the enormously respected Church leader whose Christmas messages during and immediately after the Second World War prepared the way for democratic governments throughout much of Europe.

For others of us, including Pope John Paul II, he was also the one who laid the foundations within the Catholic Church for the Second Vatican Council. His encyclical on the Church as the Mystical Body of Christ, *Mystici Corporis Christi*, 1943, opened the way for a new Catholic approach, to a theology grounded in the insights of both scripture scholars and theologians. The encyclical on biblical studies, *Divino Afflante Spiritu*, issued later in the same year, encouraged students of the written word of God to use fully the fruits of modern research. In *Mediator Dei*, 1947, Pope Pius XII set the stage for the full blossoming of the renewal of Catholic worship based on an accurate understanding of how the Church shaped her life of public prayer from the earliest Christian years. He took a first significant step in liturgical reform with the complete revision of the Holy Week Services of the Latin Church in 1956.

Between 1962 and 1965 the bishops of the Catholic world gathered as successors of the apostles around the Successors of the Apostle Peter, Blessed Pope John XXIII and Pope Paul VI, in the Second Vatican Council to shape a way of preaching the Gospel appropriate to new times. The leadership of Pope Pius XII had played a key role in preparing them and the whole Church for this moment of history.

In addition, Pope Pius XII spoke out on many issues of moral concern and of public policy: these statements laid the foundations for the Second Vatican Council's Constitution *Gaudium et Spes*, on the Church in Today's World.

In this volume Sister Margherita Marchione offers readers insights into the personal gifts Pope Pius XII brought to the service of the Church and of humanity. She cites a public record attesting to his deep commitment to the poor, the sick and afflicted, and to those especially who suffered because of the war and the ideologies that provoked it.

Sister Margherita offers us a practical understanding of how the play by the German author Hochhuth helped create in popular culture a serious misreading of a great pontiff. Certainly there is room for a wide range of informed, scholarly opinion on the record of any pontificate, especially one as long and as seriously challenged by chaotic and destructive world events as that of Pius XII. But we also need to remind ourselves that too often in our own history as a nation classic anti-Catholicism has expressed itself in attacks on the Papacy.

In these pages Sister Margherita takes us into the world of Pope Pius XII. She does so in a direct and readable way. She helps us to see how this Successor of Peter walked in the shoes of the Fisherman in troubling times with a faith that did not fail.

Cardinal WILLIAM H. KEELER
Rome, October 27, 2001

FOREWORD

Shepherd of Souls: A Pictorial Life of Pope Pius XII describes the salient periods of his pontificate and includes humorous anecdotes, historical facts, human interest stories, and revelations on the Holocaust. It captures his role as spiritual leader of the Catholic Church and celebrates his accomplishments. It is a compelling, illustrated narrative that portrays the work of the Pontiff during World War I and World War II. In particular, it contains many photographs and documents that reveal important issues of the Holocaust.

Scholars who are familiar with the attacks on Pius XII agree that he has been made a scapegoat for the crimes of others. The bottom line of vilification is that the Holocaust—the most heinous crime of recorded history—has been attributed to the Vatican. The historic evidence during Pius XII's long Pontificate testifies to his courage and integrity, as well as to his efforts to prevent the war and to shelter countless victims of the Nazis during World War II.

Sister Margherita Marchione's scholarship in the defense of Pope Pius XII began in 1997 when Paulist Press published *Yours Is a Precious Witness: Memoirs of Jews and Catholics in Wartime Italy*. This was followed by *Pope Pius XII: Architect for Peace* (2000), and *Pope Pius XII: Consensus and Controversy* (2002). In response to the careless innuendos and malicious accusations that have been leveled against Pius XII, not only did she provide the testimony of Jews and Catholics, but she has also reproduced valuable Vatican documents that help our understanding of the Holocaust.

Undoubtedly, *Shepherd of Souls: A Pictorial Life of Pope Pius XII* will help promote the truth about a saintly twentieth-century Pope.

RALPH M. CESTONE

Pope Pius XII

*Pius XII pleaded for peace: "Nothing is lost through peace; all can be lost through war."
(August 24, 1939). He denounced the war and emphasized reconciliation and a new
internal order among the various nations on Christmas Eve 1942. He revealed that
"hundreds of thousands of people, through no fault of theirs, sometimes only because
of nationality or race, were destined to die."*

CHAPTER I

The Pacelli Family

The Pacelli family arrived in Rome in 1819, from the medieval village of Viterbo, Lazio. Pope Pius XII's grandfather, Marcantonio Pacelli, was invited to Rome by His Eminence Cardinal Caterini, his maternal uncle, to study canon law and serve the Church.

By 1851 he was made Undersecretary of the Interior by Pope Pius IX. Marcantonio Pacelli was responsible for papal domains that stretched from the region of Emilia to Campania and across Italy from the Mediterranean to the Adriatic. Aware of the rapidly growing importance of the press, he co-founded *L'Osservatore Romano* in 1861. The newspaper became the voice of the Vatican. Today it continues to express the opinions of the Catholic Church.

Bedroom where the future Pope Pius XII, the third of four children, was born, March 2, 1876.

Filippo Pacelli and the former Virginia Graziosi, Eugenio's parents.

IN QVESTA CASA NACQVE

IL II MARZO MDCCCLXXVI

EVGENIO PACELLI

ELETTO PAPA

PIO XII

IL II MARZO MCMXXXIX

Plaque on the house where Pacelli was born.

Baptismal record of the Church of Saints Celsus and Julian testifying to Eugenio's baptism on March 4, 1876. His election as Pontiff was noted in the right hand margin in 1939.

Marcantonio was Undersecretary of the Interior until 1870 when the Italian government troops seized Rome after the annexation of the Papal States. This was the final step in the unification of Italy. Rome, the papal capital, now became the capital of the Italian Kingdom.

Under the "Law of Papal Guarantees" enacted in 1871, Pope Pius IX and his successors were guaranteed possession of St. Peter's, the Vatican and its gardens, the Lateran Palace, and the Villa of Castelgandolfo. Within these confines the Pope was granted sovereign rights, including the inviolability of his own person and the authority to receive and send ambassadors. He was also granted free use of the Italian telegraph, railway, and postal systems. However, Pius IX and his successors declined the annual subsidy and proclaimed themselves "prisoners of an usurping power."

Virginia Pacelli with her son Eugenio.

Marcantonio had a close, working relationship with Pope Pius IX until his death. He was present with his sons for the Pope's funeral services. Eugenio was five years old and watched the procession bearing the corpse of Pius IX to the Church of San Lorenzo. As the procession approached along the Tiber River, a mob of anticlericals rushed forth from a side street and attempted to seize the coffin and toss it into the river. Soldiers were called to quell the rioting. Charging the mob with fixed bayonets they succeeded in rescuing the coffin which was hurriedly entombed in the Church of San Lorenzo. Filippo, Eugenio's father, witnessed the scene. This incident was among Eugenio's early childhood memories.

In October 1926, to eliminate the hostility between the Church and the nation of Italy, Prime Minister Benito Mussolini began negotiations which culminated in 1929 with the signing of the Lateran Treaty. The Church was given autonomous government and legislative power as well as the right to establish its own police force, civil service, postage services, flag, currency, radio station, and a railway station. Among other concessions, papal churches, palaces, and other

Eugenio attended the elementary school of the Sisters of Divine Providence. A class picture of Eugenio and his brother, Filippo.

At age twelve, Eugenio (left) takes a break with other students during an excursion in 1888.

buildings outside the Vatican were given the territorial immunities normally reserved for foreign embassies. On February 11, 1929, Cardinal Pietro Gasparri, Vatican Secretary of State, and Mussolini signed the documents known as the Lateran Treaty. Eugenio Pacelli's brother Francesco, a brilliant Vatican lawyer, is credited with helping to negotiate the Lateran Treaty with the Italian Government.

The Vatican was now an independent sovereign state. Pope Pius XI was pleased with the way the Treaty was written and stated: "We have given back God to Italy and Italy to God." Catholics throughout the world agreed with this assessment.

Early Years

The Pacelli family lived in a twelve-room apartment on the third floor of a four-story brownstone building called Palazzo Pediconi, across the Tiber from St. Peter's, at Number 34 Via degli Orsini, the palace built centuries earlier by the Orsini family.

Grandfather Marcantonio had seven children, of whom the third son was Filippo, who married Virginia

Fifteen-year-old Eugenio at the Liceo Quirino Visconti (2ⁿᵈ row, 2ⁿᵈ from right).

At eighteen, Eugenio entered Almo Collegio Capranica to study for the priesthood.

Graziosi. They had four children. Eugenio, their second son and third child, became Pope Pius XII. The older Pacelli boy was Francesco. The two sisters were Giuseppina and Elisabetta. They and Francesco married distinguished Romans and had six children among them. Their offspring, ten grandnieces and grand-nephews, were the children for whom a Christmas tree was arranged in the papal apartment and their uncle, Pope Pius XII, gave them presents on Christmas Day.

Eugenio Maria Giuseppe Giovanni Pacelli was born in Rome, March 2, 1876, and baptized two days later, according to the records at the Church of Saints Celso and Giuliano. He was baptized by his uncle, Monsignor Giuseppe Pacelli. His godparents were his maternal uncle Filippo Graziosi and paternal aunt Teresa Pacelli.

The Seminary was called "A factory of Cardinals." Those that can be identified are (from left): first, Cardinal Luigi Maglione; fourth, Cardinal Clemente Micara; fifth, Cardinal Francesco Marchetti Selvaggiani; sixth, Pius XII; ninth, Cardinal Benedetto Aloisi Masella. The others may well have followed ecclesiastical careers, as the eighth, Monsignor Carlo Respighi who became the Prefect of Ceremonies.

Pope Pius XII visits the Seminary in 1957.

A few years later, the Pacellis moved to Number 20, Via della Vetrina. Eugenio enjoyed a childhood in deeply religious surroundings. In the apartment there was a shrine of the Madonna with a prie-dieu where he would kneel and pray.

This new residence was fortunately nearer the kindergarten and elementary school conducted by the Sisters of Divine Providence. At age four Eugenio was enrolled in this school. In 1939, when a bust of Pius XII was unveiled at the school and the newly-elected Pope took the opportunity to praise his loving mother and the devoted and gifted nuns for instilling in him the "first principles of Christian piety."

Eugenio was a precocious child, sensitive and impressionable. He was deeply impressed as he listened to his mother explaining the lives of the saints and the early martyrs of the Church. One day, his uncle Monsignor Giuseppe Pacelli told him the

story of a missionary priest who was persecuted and finally crucified by his tormentors. Eugenio told his uncle, that he too would like to be a martyr, "but—without the nails."

After kindergarten and elementary school, Eugenio began his studies at the Ennio Quirino Visconti Lyceum. When classes at the Lyceum were over each day, young Eugenio would wait for his brother Francesco in the Church of the Gesù. Questioned by his mother about why he went to the church, he said simply, "I talk to our Lady."

It was here that he established a close friendship with a Jewish schoolmate, Guido Mendes. The boys visited each other's home and shared common interests. Still vivid in 1958 in the elderly Mendes' memory were the strong anti-church and anti-clerical prejudices rampant among Italian schools and teachers in the 1890's.

17

Pacelli was ordained a priest on April 2, 1899, and celebrated his first Mass in the Basilica of Saint Mary Major.

He remembered his classmate Eugenio always speaking up to defend the Church. He described Eugenio as a careful dresser, always wearing a coat and tie, and distinguishing himself as the leading student. "He was always winning academic prizes," Mendes recalled. He also stated that when the Fascists began to threaten Jews in Italy, the then Secretary of State Pacelli helped the Mendes family flee to Jerusalem. They remained in touch with one another over the years.

Other classmates remember the time one of his professors asked the class to write an essay on the greatest leaders of all time. Eugenio wrote about Saint Augustine. The teacher was amused and asked ironically who could possibly make a case for Augustine, the self-confessed sinner. Pacelli stood up. "I can. Any time you are ready to listen. For one thing, the Bishop of Hippo repented." The teacher had no answer in the face of the teenage boy's informed and sensible statement.

Around this same time, when assigned to write a composition about how much good had been achieved for Italy with the seizure of the Papal States, Eugenio roundly condemned the move as plain robbery and persecution. He might well have been expelled from school for such anti-nationalist sentiments, but his teachers thought him too intelligent and talented to be dismissed.

Throughout his life, he had a phenomenal memory, not just in Italian but in any one of the many languages at his command. He had no difficulty learning Latin. As an altar boy, Eugenio willingly accepted the challenge of getting up early for the first Mass of the day. But, like most very young boys, neatness was not a priority. One day, as a Cardinal, he visited the Chiesa Nuova and wandered into the sacristy where he had been an altar boy. Pointing his finger at a wall, he remarked: "There is the hook toward which I used to fling collar, tie, and cassock before running home. They didn't always make the hook."

Pacelli had many hobbies. He was a natural for dramatics. His teachers recognized his ability to speak and captivate an audience. Summers were spent at their family home in Onano, where he liked to ride his horse. He was also a good swimmer in Lake Bolsena and he was swift and tireless as a canoeist. As a hiker he had the reputation of being unbeatable. His collection of coins and stamps was admired by his friends. From an early age he maintained an ardent interest in Archaeology, and carefully searched out and studied inscriptions of early Christians in the Catacombs.

Young Violinist

Eugenio's education was strict and demanding. Records show that he was at the top of every class he attended, and he graduated with highest honors. His memory was phenomenal, he possessed what today would be called a photographic memory—the ability to comprehend and retain pages of any book he read with great rapidity.

After a four-day retreat, Pacelli announced to his family that he would not follow family tradition and become a lawyer, but that he intended to become a priest.

The announcement came as no surprise. The Pacellis knew that Eugenio had always been a serious, deeply committed and religious young boy and teenager. In 1894, at the age of 18, he entered the Capranica Seminary and enrolled at the Gregorian University. Not by nature physically robust, he taxed his body with prodigious study and prayers. At an early age he was afflicted with stomach difficulties that never disappeared and early on there were signs of tuberculosis. For these reasons, thanks to Pope Leo XIII who came to his rescue, Eugenio was given permission to live at home while he continued his courses at the Sapienza School of Philosophy and Letters, as well as at the Papal Athenaeum of St. Apollinaris for Theology. This was an unprecedented dispensation. He progressed rapidly through his studies and received his Baccalaureate and Licentiate degrees *summa cum laude*. His frail health prevented his participation at the graduation ceremony. He was ordained a priest on Easter Sunday, April 2, 1899, in Bishop Francesco Paolo Cassetta's private chapel. The next day, Eugenio Pacelli celebrated his first Mass in the Borghese Chapel of the Basilica of Saint Mary Major, in Rome.

As a boy, Eugenio loved to play the violin. He was exceptionally talented and often the entire family enjoyed listening while he played and his sisters accompanied him on the mandolin. As a young priest he would, whenever his pressing studies and duties allowed, refresh his soul by playing the violin. It was during one of these occasions that the then Monsignor Pietro Gasparri came to give him some very important news. He told him that the Vatican was impressed with his abilities and wanted him to take an apprentice position in the Vatican's Secretariat of State. Pacelli lowered his violin and said: "But I had hoped to spend my life as a shepherd of souls." Little did Father Pacelli then know that he was destined to be the Church's supreme shepherd of souls.

Even as a young man, Eugenio Pacelli showed interest and concern in nature and for all God's creatures. This affinity continued when he became Pope. At the farm in Castelgandolfo, he would walk about simply enjoying the presence of the animals, especially the sheep, which he often gently touched. Later, when he was in the Vatican he would take brisk walks each day beneath the cypresses and pines, pausing to admire the beautiful flowers in the Vatican gardens.

Though as Pope he would usually eat his meals alone, that changed somewhat one day after the papal gardener found a helpless bird, which had been injured in the garden. Knowing the Pontiff's love for nature, the gardener brought the bird to his apartment. Pacelli was fascinated, helped nurse the bird back to health and decided to keep it in his apartment. He named her, Gretel. As soon as she was fully recovered, she was given several companions. While the Pope ate, the birds were released from their cages. Twittering, the birds would perch on his shoulder or on the table where they had their own small dishes of seeds. Thereafter at mealtime he was vicariously back in the natural world he knew in the summers of his youth.

Pius XII visits the Capranica Seminary.

20

CHAPTER II

Priestly Career

Father Eugenio Pacelli's first assignment was as a curate at Chiesa Nuova, the church where he had served as an altar boy. While there, he taught catechism to the children who loved him because he was gentle, kind, patient and understanding. At the same time he pursued his studies for a doctorate in Canon Law and Civil Law at the Apollinaris. Incredibly, only two years later, he would add doctorates in Philosophy and in Theology.

Some indication of the esteem in which young Pacelli was held by the leaders of the Church at the end of the 19th and the beginning of the 20th century is indicated by the fact that he was selected for a very delicate diplomatic mission in 1901. In that year Queen Victoria died, and Pope Leo XIII sent Father Pacelli to London with a personal handwritten letter of condolence for her son, King Edward VII.

In 1904, Father Pacelli became a Papal Chamberlain with the title of Monsignor and one year later a Domestic Prelate. The reception of all these honors did not keep the new Monsignor from continuing to teach catechism to children in one of Rome's poorest quarters, or from conducting spiritual conferences for the French Sisters of Namur who ran an academy for girls of the Roman aristocracy. All this time he counseled working girls who

Pacelli's First Mass was announced in the *L'Osservatore Romano*.

List of Masses celebrated.

21

On October 3, 1903, Professor D. Eugenio Pacelli was assigned to the Secretariat of State.

resided at the House of Saint Rose in spiritual matters. His own spiritual life continued to be intense and exemplary. In addition to morning meditation and Mass, Pacelli always managed to find two hours a day to spend on his knees before the Blessed Sacrament. It would be a pattern he would follow his entire llife.

Pacelli was again sent to England in 1908, where he attended the Eucharistic Congress in London. The 32-year-old priest was by that time well embarked

Pacelli was sent to London in 1910.

Pope Benedict XV consecrates Monsignor Pacelli a Bishop on May 13, 1917, in the Sistine Chapel.

He is present for the signing of the Concordat with Serbia.

on what would become a nearly 40-year career of brilliant diplomatic service for the Church. From 1904 to 1916, he was a research aide in the Office of the Congregation of Extraordinary Ecclesiastical Affairs where he assisted Cardinal Pietro Gasparri in the crucial task of clarifying and updating canon law.

In 1910, Monsignor Pacelli was again back in London where he represented the Holy See at the Coronation of King George V. This trip demonstrated some remarkable ingenuity on his part. While unpacking, he discovered that a bottle of iodine in his toilet kit had spilled on the pope's salutation to the new monarch. Pacelli made the best of what must have seemed a disastrous accident. He calmly swabbed more iodine over the entire document before presenting it to the king. It seemed to the monarch and to all who looked at the document as though it had been written on extremely ancient papal parchment.

In 1911, Pius X appointed Pacelli Undersecretary for Extraordinary Ecclesiastical Affairs. This department of the Secretariat of State negotiated terms of agreements with foreign governments that would allow the Church to carry out its teaching mission. In 1912, he was appointed Pro-Secretary. Two years later, he became Secretary of the Congregation of Extraordinary Ecclesiastical Affairs.

Difficulties in Germany

In 1914, Pius X died and Benedict XV was called to the Chair of Peter. On April 20, 1917, the new Pope appointed Monsignor Pacelli as Nuncio to Bavaria, Germany, a nation on the verge of military defeat and revolutionary chaos. Before assuming

Pacelli was Archbishop of the titular See of Sardi. He presented Benedict XV's peace proposals to the Kaiser and dedicated himself to the assistance of prisoners of war.

full responsibilities in Germany, Pacelli was consecrated a Bishop by Pope Benedict XV in the Sistine Chapel (May 13, 1917). Present were Pacelli's mother, father, brother and sisters and five Cardinals. He was then elevated to the rank of Archbishop and went to Germany to present his credentials to Ludwig III, King of Bavaria on May 28, 1917.

When he visited Kaiser Wilhelm II, Archbishop Pacelli begged him to do all in his power to end World War I. In his diary the Prussian wrote that he "liked the man from Rome well enough as a human being. But this was war. Let the British and French answer for it." Benedict XV's proposals for peaceful settlement were not accepted.

The Kaiser thought that the collapse of the Russian army meant that the Germans could now concentrate on the French and British and quickly achieve victory. He had not calculated the impact of America's entering the war. As World War I continued on all fronts

with renewed fury, the young Nuncio dedicated himself to tending to the spiritual and physical assistance of the sick and wounded men in hospitals and to assisting prisoners of war in their camps and in their attempts to communicate with their families. After the war his reputation grew among both civil and ecclesiastical authorities. Field Marshall Paul von Hindenburg, who was president of Germany from 1925 to 1934, wrote of "the noble conception Archbishop Pacelli had of his office, his wise objectivity, his inflexible sense of justice, his generous humanity, and his great love for his neighbor."

American newspaper and radio commentator Dorothy Thompson, wrote: "Those of us who were foreign correspondents in Berlin during the days of the Weimar Republic were not unfamiliar with the figure of the dean of the diplomatic corps. Tall, slender, with magnificent eyes, strong features and expressive hands, in his appearance and bearing

Pope Pius XII.

Archbishop Pacelli looked every inch what he was—a Roman nobleman, of the proudest blood of the western world. In knowledge of German and European affairs and in diplomatic astuteness the Nuncio was without an equal."

Archbishop Pacelli's mother passed away in the winter of 1917. The following spring his father followed her. Such personal sorrow affected his own health. He contacted a flu-like illness and desperately needed rest and care. Arrangements were made for him to recuperate in a convent in Einsiedeln, Switzerland. Gradually he regained his health. One day, while walking to a village near the convent, he met a little boy crying and tried to console him. He learned that the toddler had lost money his mother had given him to buy bread. The Nuncio dried the youngster's tears, bought the bread, and walked the child home. Soon after, Pacelli resumed his duties in Munich.

After the war, the papacy turned the attention of the Allied powers to the great dangers that would arise "unless a peace which Germans can accept and which is not humiliating for them... is reached." Most Germans found it difficult to live with the Treaty of Versailles of 1919. If not accepted, the Allies stated, it would mean the resumption of their military operations. Among those who objected most indignantly to the re-birth of Poland was General von Seeckt, a power in the re-birth of the vanquished German army, who stated in 1922: "Poland's existence is intolerable and incompatible with the essential conditions of Germany's life. Poland must go and will go... The obliteration of Poland must be one of the fundamental drives of German policy."[1]

An incident demonstrating Pacelli's support for a democratic-republican government took place in Munich in 1922. At a hostile political meeting, Konrad Adenauer, who later became Chancellor of the West German Republic, defended republicanism as the best hope for Germany. His audience favored the monarchy. When Adenauer finished his speech,

Nuncio Pacelli distributes packages to prisoners of war in Germany during World War I.

Nunzio Pacelli participates in a procession in Rottenburg after the war.

In 1927, Archbishop Pacelli visited the Gelsenkircen mine in the Ruhr.

only Eugenio Pacelli, the Papal Nuncio, clapped his hands enthusiastically.

Regardless of his private convictions, Pacelli saw republicanism as good for Germany. Therefore, when Bishop Michael von Faulhaber rose for a rebuttal of Adenauer's arguments, Pacelli jerked at Faulhaber's cassock. The Bishop was surprised but he sat down and went along with the diplomatic intuitions of the Papal Nuncio.

Pacelli's support for democracy was rooted in the laws of God as he explained in his 1944 Christmas address and later demonstrated by encouraging the Christian Democrats in Italy after World War II. Years later, when a visitor asked him what the Vatican thought of a complex international situation, Pius XII responded: "I am not the Vatican, my son; I am only the Pope."

Only Weapon: The Cross

For decades Pacelli confronted world problems. On June 22, 1920, Pacelli became the first Apostolic

Nuncio to Germany. Four years later, March 29, 1924, he signed a concordat with Bavaria which was ratified by its Parliament, January 15, 1925. It determined the rights and duties of the Church and the government in respect to each other. After concluding a concordat with Bavaria, Pacelli was able to succeed with Prussia and Baden, but had no success with either the Reich or the Soviet Union. After some time in Munich, the Apostolic Nuncio's residence was transferred to Berlin. His peace efforts did not succeed. The Germans were not ready for peace. As Nuncio and then as Vatican Secretary of State, Pacelli faced and feared the rise of the National Socialists.

Ever since the defeat of Germany when Communist mobs seized control of Munich in February 1919, the diplomatic corps from every country returned to safety, except Pacelli, who continued his errands of mercy toward the desperate public. The Bolsheviks began a campaign of hate against Archbishop Pacelli. Armed terrorists penetrated the nunciature and, pointing a pistol at the Nunzio, demanded that he surrender his car.

Pacelli refused. Tall and defiant, he slowly descended the stairs, stating: "You must leave at once! This house does not belong to the government, but to the Holy See. It is inviolable under international law." As he held his pectoral cross, the socialist leader stepped forward, jamming his gun against the Archbishop's chest. But the gun muzzle glanced off the pectoral cross and, seeing what he had struck, the man wavered and left without harming the Nunzio.

Shortly after this incident, while delivering food and medical supplies to a center for children dying of starvation, another mob attacked Pacelli's car. The Nuncio ordered the chauffeur to stop the car and put down the top. Holding the Cross high above his head for all to see, he blessed the mob. "My mission is peace," he said. "The only weapon we have is this Cross... Why should you harm us?" Slowly, the crowd dispersed. (Years later during a TV program, Bishop Fulton Sheen repeated this story, adding: "The cross Pacelli wore that day, is the cross I am now wearing!" He had received it as a token of the Pope's esteem.)

In 1929, Archbishop Pacelli was named a Cardinal. The following year he succeeded Cardinal Gasparri as Vatican Secretary of State.

CHAPTER III

Anti-Semitic Persecution

The Lateran Treaty of 1929 established formal relations between Italy and the Vatican. Following the example of Mussolini, Adolf Hitler initiated a Concordat. This is a strictly defined legal agreement between two governments intended to preserve the freedom of the Church to teach and minister to the faithful. Historically the Holy See has signed many such agreements. There was nothing unique about the Concordats with Italy in 1929 or with Germany in 1933. In fact, Pacelli negotiated a concordat with Bavaria which was signed on March 29, 1924 and concluded one with Prussia on June 14, 1929. Pacelli was then recalled to Rome and on December 16, received a Cardinal's hat. Soon after, February 7, 1930, he was appointed Secretary of State (succeeding his former mentor Cardinal Pietro Gasparri) and became archpriest of the Vatican Basilica.

Cardinal Pacelli negotiated with the Germans to protect the rights of Catholics. The Holy See agreed because the new German regime was determined to tamper with the existing Concordats with Bavaria and Prussia.

Opposed to Nazi ideology, the Church could yet register protests and keep its independence. As long as the German government guaranteed freedom of religion, the Catholic Church could express its point of view. However, the Holy See had to make concessions. Only party members were allowed to engage in politics. The Catholic clergy could no longer participate. Soon after, the official Protestant Church came under Nazi influence and a *Reichsbischof* was appointed.

The National Socialist Party exploited all the problems and fears of Germans to their own purpose, promising to achieve national unity, to undo the "shame" of Versailles, and to make Germany

Cardinal Pacelli is named Archpriest of St. Peter's Basilica.

At the entrance to the Nunziature in Munich.

great again. The party vowed to fight Communism and any form of Marxism.

President Hindenburg, who for many years had refused to appoint Adolf Hitler as Chancellor, succumbed to the opposition on January 30, 1933. In replacing Franz von Papen, a former Catholic Center Party member, Hitler became the leader of the largest party in the *Reichstag*.

Jewish descendants, even if baptized, were deprived of their German citizenship. In 1934, when the Nazis initiated their first large-scale massacre, Cardinal Pacelli had the Vatican newspaper unequivocally condemn the Nazi crimes.

"The *Osservatore*," wrote French correspondent Charles Pichon, "in three articles, proclaimed that National Socialism better deserved the name of 'national terrorism,' and that like all movements which resort to terrorism, it sprang from a gang rather than from a party."[2]

The Nazi government now engaged in open warfare against the Church. In fact, Hitler's principal collaborator, Martin Bormann, declared: "We

As Secretary of State, Pacelli signs the Concordat with Berlin.

34

Papal Legate in Budapest.

Germans, are the first to be appointed by destiny to break with Christianity. It will be an honor for us. A thousand ties link us to the Christian faith; they will be broken with a single blow. Our intention is not to raze the cathedrals to the ground, but to fill them with a new ideology and with proclamations of a new faith."[3]

In a letter dated March 12, 1935 to Cardinal Schulte of Cologne, Pacelli attacked the Nazis as "false prophets with the pride of Lucifer," labeling them "bearers of a new faith and a new gospel" who were attempting to create a "mendacious antinomy between faithfulness to the Church and to the Fatherland."[4]

As Papal Legate, Pacelli presides at the Eucharistic Congress in Budapest.

The following month, Cardinal Pacelli delivered an address before a quarter of a million people at Lourdes, April 25-28, 1935, where he described the Nazis as "possessed by the superstition of race and blood" and declared that "the Church does not consent to form a compact with them at any price." Describing the speech, the *New York Times* headlined its story: "Nazis Warned at Lourdes" (April 29, 1935). French newspapers at the time were ecstatic over Pacelli's visit and were praising him as the most brilliant churchman in memory.

Visit to the USA

Cardinal Pacelli represented Pope Pius XI on many occasions. He was sent to Buenos Aires, Argentina, aboard the *Conte Grande* and presided as Papal Legate at the International Eucharistic Congress, October 10-14, 1934. He was also Pope Pius XI's delegate to France for the closing days of the Jubilee Year honoring the nineteenth centenary of Redemption. In 1936 he visited the United States of America.

Planes accompanied the *Conte di Savoia*, October 8, 1936, as the ship sailed down the New York Harbor and passed the Statue of Liberty. Cardinal

Present site of Vatican Radio Station.

Cardinal Pacelli with Pope Pius XI and Guglielmo Marconi during a visit to the site of Vatican Radio.

Eugenio Pacelli was a Vatican representative. During the official salute, fireboats sprayed the harbor with multicolored streams; warships fired volley after volley high into the sky; sailboats, steamers, yachts, barges, rowboats proudly showed the papal colors of yellow and white.

Upon his arrival in New York, Cardinal Pacelli was met by over fifty journalists and photographers. Pacelli stated: "I am indeed happy to find myself within the territory of a great people who know how to unite so beautifully and so nobly a sense of discipline and the exercise of a just, legitimate and well-ordered liberty." Smiling happily, he walked down the gangway determined to see America as a tourist.

The trip was billed as a vacation for Cardinal Pacelli, but reporters felt the Vatican Secretary of State came to silence the radio priest, Father Charles E. Coughlin and take the Catholic Church out of the American presidential campaign. Bishop Francis Spellman arranged for Cardinal Pacelli to be the guest of Nicholas Brady's wife, Papal Duchess Genevieve Brady, at Inisfada, her Long Island residence in Manhasset, New York.

Pacelli made contact with every aspect of American life. His first stop was to St. Patrick's Cathedral in Manhattan and the residence of Patrick Cardinal Hayes. There he lunched with Nicholas Murray Butler, President of Columbia University. He visited the Empire State Building and admired the skyline of New York and in Philadelphia he saw the Liberty Bell. He had a whirlwind tour of the United States: Cleveland, Chicago, Notre Dame, San Francisco, Boulder Dam,

Minneapolis, Kansas City. At Notre Dame University Pacelli received an honorary LL.D.

The children of Sacred Heart School in Massachusetts presented a special program in honor of Cardinal Pacelli. He congratulated them in English concluding with: "I wish to tell you that I thoroughly enjoyed it. I realize that you must have worked very hard. And therefore I grant you two holidays, today and tomorrow." Remembering his own school days, he accepted the thunderous applause as gratitude for the free days rather than tribute to himself.

Among other stops he visited Richard Cardinal Cushing in Boston and the Knights of Columbus head-

In 1934, Cardinal Pacelli was the Papal Legate to the 32nd International Eucharistic Congress in Buenos Aires.

In 1935, Cardinal Pacelli was the Papal Legate to Lourdes, to officiate at the closing celebrations of the Holy Year.

In 1936, Cardinal Pacelli traveled aboard the "Conte di Savoia" for an "unofficial visit" to the United States.

Pacelli visits Washington's home in Mount Vernon, Virginia.

At the Museum in Mount Vernon, Pacelli stands between Bishop Spellman and Bishop Amleto Cicognani, Apostolic Delegate to the USA.

At prayer in the chapel of Notre Dame University, Indiana.

In procession with Cardinal Hayes in the Cathedral of New York.

Cardinal Pacelli during his whirlwind trip to the USA at Roosevelt Field, New York.

form stood on each side of the pathway, every five feet, all the way to the Gymnasium, where over 5,000 guests were seated. Church dignitaries and distinguished guests followed in procession. Cameras and sound equipment recorded the proceedings. The Columbia network carried the Cardinal's voice on a coast-to-coast hook-up, and millions of people throughout the country were able to see and hear the memorable ceremony. The Fordham University Glee Club presented a magnificent performance.

Addressing the audience, President Robert I. Gannon, S.J., stated: "Fordham University has never been more honored or more humanly pleased by any academic event in its history of a hundred years." He made reference to the fact that the name Pacelli suggests peace; that the motto on his crest—*opus justitiae pax*—was indeed meaningful; that it is in the universities where the love of justice flourish-

On October 13, Pacelli visits the Knights of Columbus headquarters in New Haven, Connecticut. Seated from left to rigiht: Bishop Francis J. Spellman, Cardinal Pacelli, Supreme Knight Martin Carmody. Standing: John Conway, William J. McGinley, Enrico Galeazzi, representative of the Knights in Rome.

quarters in New Haven, Connecticut. On October 21 he went to Baltimore and was welcomed by Archbishop Michael Curley, as he visited the Cathedral of the Assumption and St. Mary's Seminary, both the oldest in the United States. The next day he went to Washington, DC, and made the following stops: the Catholic University, the National Catholic Welfare Conference, and Georgetown University where he received the honorary degree of doctor of canon and civil law. At the Library of Congress, he was interested in seeing the Declaration of Independence, the Constitution and an original score of Abbé Franz Liszt, the Hungarian pianist and composer. He signed the guest register "E. Card. Pacelli." That same day he visited Mount Vernon, the home and tombs of George and Martha Washington where he placed memorial wreaths.

Fordham University

On Sunday afternoon, November 1, 1936, Fordham University held a special convocation in honor of His Eminence Eugenio Cardinal Pacelli, Secretary of State to His Holiness Pope Pius XI. With the University Band leading the procession from Keating Hall, the entire R.O.T.C. Unit, in column formation, marched past His Eminence, and then formed a guard of honor. To welcome Cardinal Pacelli, a man in uni-

42

es. President Gannon referred to the issue of pacifism that was raising havoc among American students: "For pacifism is to the true love of peace what prohibition is to temperance. …For there is no peace without justice and no justice without truth, so that a university which devotes itself to the truth is a strong defense for peace in both State and Church."

After his gracious acceptance of the honorary degree, Cardinal Pacelli spoke about the need for education "which develops the whole man, morally as well as intellectually, spiritually as well as scientifically, an education that rests upon the rock of truth and not upon the sand of mere materialism, a truly Christian education illumined by the light of faith. … Your university is rich in promise for the future because you cherish the precious heritage of the past… Be true to the traditions of your Alma Mater and be not drawn away from those time honored studies which have made saints and scholars in the Old World, and in the New World have produced leaders of men, loyal to God and to country, the strongest bulwark of the nation." The applause was enthusiastic!

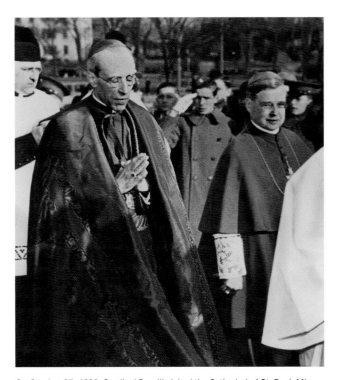

On October 27, 1936, Cardinal Pacelli visited the Cathedral of St. Paul, Minnesota. To his right is Archbishop John Gregory Murray.

On November 1st, Cardinal Pacelli visits the Catholic University, Washington, DC. He is greeted by Father Roth, O.P.

43

Cardinal Pacelli visits the Library of Congress, Washington, DC., and admires the Gutenberg Bible. Standing next to the Cardinal is the librarian, Herbert Putnam.

Monsignor LaValle, Bishop Spellman, Cardinal Pacelli, Bishop Kearney, and Bishop Walsh of Maryknoll.

Cardinal Pacelli receives a degree Honoris Causa at Fordham University, Bronx, NY.

Joseph P. Kennedy (left) and Marvin McIntyre (right), FDR's presidential secretary, officially welcome Eugenio Cardinal Pacelli to President Roosevelt's home in Hyde Park.

Cardinal Pacelli then faced the student body to grant the customary day off. With a radiant smile, he announced: "I grant you a holi-day." The word he pronounced with a slight Italian accent sounded like "holy day." There was no reaction from the students and no one applauded. The silence alarmed the Cardinal, so he waved his hands in the air, shouting: "Free day!" "Free day!" This time his message sounded like "three days." The applause was deafening! The *faux pas* was later straightened out, but it was never forgotten.

Cardinal Eugenio Pacelli had a wonderful sense of humor. A few years later, on March 2, 1939, he was elected to the Papacy and became Pope Pius XII, the Vicar of Christ on earth. Whenever visitors came from Fordham University, Pius XII asked: "Do you remember my terrible mistake? Can you ever forgive me?"

Return to the Vatican

Eugneio Pacelli was seen by more people and was the most accessible Pope in the history of the papacy up to his pontificate. Americans were awed into silence by his presence. Thousands were able to greet him as he traveled aboard United Airlines DC-3. Boarding at Roosevelt Field, Long Island, Cardinal Pacelli crisscrossed the United States. He worked far into the night inspiring one hostess to state: "He was the most considerate passenger I ever had. He was Christ-like."

This was an "unofficial" trip covering some eight thousand miles in seven days chiefly by chartered plane of the United Airlines over congested cities, rocky mountains and flat lands. In San Francisco he blessed the Golden Gate Bridge. During the tour, Captain Jack O'Brien was the pilot, and the stewardess was Miss Madeline Quirici, who spoke both English and Italian. The Vatican Secretary of State made an in-depth study of the American Church. He also appealed to the United States to throw open its doors to Jewish refugees, but his request went unheeded. On November 5, 1936, the eve of his return to the Vatican, President Franklin D. Roosevelt—who two days earlier had a landslide victory for a second term—invited Cardinal Pacelli to a luncheon at his home in Hyde Park, New York. He was given a warm reception. On the return to New York City, Pacelli was delighted when, visiting Ambassador Joseph P. Kennedy's family in Bronxville, five-year-old Teddy climbed on his lap and had him open the gift that the Cardinal had given him.

As Cardinal Pacelli and representatives of the clergy and laity crossed Manhattan to board the ship at Pier 59 on the North River for his return voyage, he gave a written statement to the press which included the following: "I am leaving America with sorrow, and yet with gratitude in my heart to all with whom I have come in contact, and with the prayer that Almighty God may continue to bless this great nation, that its citizens may be happy and prosperous and that the influence of the United States may always be exerted for the promotion of peace among peoples." As the color guard dipped the flags of the United States and the Holy See, the *Conte di Savoia* moved out into the river. It reached Naples on November 14. The Cardinal took a train for Rome, motored to Vatican City and met for two hours with Pope Pius XI, giving him a detailed report on his journey.

Papal Encyclical

In his encyclical *Mit brennender Sorge*, Pope Pius XI condemned anti-Semitism: "None but superficial minds could stumble into concepts of a national God, of a national religion; or attempt to lock within the frontiers of a single people, within the narrow limits of a single race, God, the Creator of the universe, King and Legislator of all nations before whose immensity they are 'as a drop of a bucket' (Isaiah XI, 15)."

Pacelli meets with British Ministers Neville Chamberlain and Lord Halifax on January 13, 1939.

The encyclical, prepared under the direction of Cardinal Pacelli, then Secretary of State, was written in German for wider dissemination in that country. It was smuggled out of Italy, copied and distributed to parish priests to be read from all of the pulpits on Palm Sunday, March 21, 1937.

No one who heard the Pontifical document had any illusion about the gravity of these statements or their significance. Certainly the Nazis understood their important message. An internal German memorandum dated March 23, 1937 stated that it was "almost a call to do battle against the Reich government." The encyclical, *Mit brennender Sorge*, was confiscated, printers arrested and presses seized. The following day *Das Schwarze Korps* called it "the most incredible of Pius XI's pastoral letters: every sentence in it was an insult to the new Germany."

Cardinal Pacelli returned to France in 1937, as Cardinal-Legate to consecrate and dedicate the new basilica in Lisieux during the Eucharistic Congress and made another anti-Nazi statement. He again presided on May 25-30, 1938, at the International Eucharistic Congress in Budapest.

Before entering the Conclave.

47

Count Galeazzo Ciano, Italy's foreign minister, with Cardinal Pacelli and other Church dignitaries assembled at the Sistine Chapel in February 1939 to pay homage to the deceased Pope Pius XI.

Prince Umberto expresses the condolence of the Royal Family. With him are Cardinal Pacelli, Granito di Belmonte and Nasalli Rocca.

CHAPTER IV

Election of Pope Pius XII

On February 28, 1939 the *New York Times* reported: "The Jewish issue in Italy is growing more intense and is one of the gravest of the many serious problems being considered by the Cardinals who will enter the conclave...to elect a new Pope."[5]

The Cardinals elected Eugenio Pacelli—the 262nd Pope—on his sixty-third birthday, March 2, 1939. He received sixty-one out of the sixty-two votes because he did not vote for himself, and was elected

Pontiff. He selected the name of his predecessor Pius XI, and became Pope Pius XII. The bells of Saint Peter's pealed on March 12, 1939, as the eyes of countless people turned toward the balcony.

Dressed in a white cope and wearing a silver, gem-studded mitre on his head Pope Pius XII appeared. Cardinal Nicola Canali removed the mitre. Cardinal Camillo Caccia-Dominioni replaced it with the papal tiara and prayed: "Receive the tiara adorned with the three crowns and know that you are the Father of princes and kings, the Sovereign of the world, and the Vicar on earth of our Savior Jesus

Summoned to the Vatican Conclave, the Sacred College of Cardinals elected Eugenio Cardinal Pacelli, March 2, 1939.

Procession in the Basilica.

Pope Pius XII blesses thousands in St. Peter's Square.

Christ, to Whom is honor and glory, now and forever. Amen."

Pope Pius XII's coat-of-arms showed the symbol of peace: a dove with an olive branch. His motto indicated peace to be a fruit of justice: *Opus justitiae pax* (Is. 34, 17). His first radio message to the world was, "Peace, gift of God, desired by all upright men, the fruit of love and justice." He was a man of peace.

Immediately after his election, Pius XII issued a call for a peace conference of European leaders. Documents show that in a last minute bid to avert bloodshed, the Pope called for a conference involving Italy, France, England, Germany and Poland. Pius XII's peace plan was based on five points: the defense of small nations, the right to life, disarma-

ment, some new kind of League of Nations and a plea for the moral principles of justice and love. Through his public discourses, his appeals to governments, and his secret diplomacy, he was engaged more than any other individual in the effort to avert war and rebuild peace. His request went unheeded.

Pius XII then met with the German Cardinals who had been present in the recent conclave, in order to ascertain the real situation of the Church in Nazi Germany. These meetings provided him with direct proof and information that motivated the content of his first encyclical, *Summi Pontificatus*.

Dated October 20, 1939, this encyclical was a strong attack on totalitarianism. In it, Pius XII singled out those governments, who by their deifica-

The ceremony of his coronation took place on March 12, 1939.

Cardinal Nicola Canali removed the mitre. Cardinal Camillo Caccia-Dominioni replaced it with the papal tiara.

After his coronation, the voice of Pius XII rang out across St. Peter's Square in a blessing on the city and on the world.

Pius XII speaks from the papal throne.

tion of the state, imperiled the spirit of humanity. He spoke about restoring the foundation of human society to its origin in natural law, to its source in Christ, the only true ruler of all men and women of all nations and races.

In this encyclical Pius XII reprimanded: "What age has been, for all its technical and purely civic progress, more tormented than ours by spiritual emptiness and deep-felt interior poverty?" The world had abandoned Christ's cross for another [the Swastika] which brings only death. The consecration of the world to Christ the King celebrates "a penetrating wisdom which sets itself to restore and to ennoble all human society and to promote its true welfare." Indeed, Pius XII's encyclicals, discourses and radio messages clearly assert that the only solid foundation for social order is the law of God.

World War II

The Catholic Church is not a political institution but a spiritual one whose mission is to obtain the eternal salvation of all men, of every race and country. The traditional policy of the Church in time of war is impartiality. She cannot ally herself with or against any nation or nations. She must tell the nations of the world what Christian morality per-

mits and forbids; she must condemn crimes against justice and charity; she must ease the sufferings of the war's victims. Although neutral as to the political aspects of war, the Church is belligerent as to its moral aspects.

On the eve of World War II, the international position of the Vatican was dangerous and difficult. The anti-Semitic decrees enacted by Mussolini in 1938 were causing bitter conflicts between Italy and the Holy See.

As a diplomat, Pius XII saw war approaching and instructed the papal representatives to Germany, Italy, France, Poland and England to learn whether mediation by the Pope would be considered. He tried to awaken in world leaders the full realization of what they were about to do.

On August 24, 1939 he gave each papal representative the text of a speech asking them to convey it to their respective governments. That evening he read the speech to the world: "The danger is imminent, but there is still time. Nothing is lost with peace; all can be lost with war. Let men return to

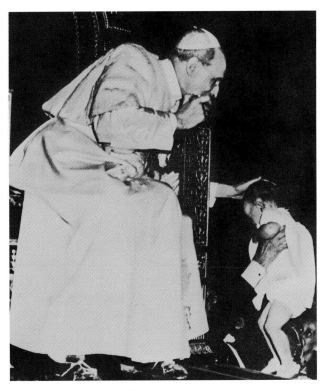

He bends down to bless a child.

55

Pius XII prepares for a papal ceremony.

mutual understanding! Let them begin negotiations anew, conferring with good will and with respect for reciprocal rights…"

Without interruption before and during the war, Pius XII continued his work for peace, striving to heal the wounds inflicted by this great tragedy. The papacy rescued Jews by channeling money to those in need, issuing countless baptismal certificates for their protection, negotiating with Latin American countries to grant them visas, and keeping in touch with their relatives through the Vatican Information Service.

During the North African campaign a boatload of Allied wounded arrived in Italy for hospitalization and imprisonment. A Vatican representative boarded the boat and distributed message forms among the soldiers who immediately filled, signed and addressed them. Within weeks after their capture the families of these American soldiers received information sent airmail by the Vatican to the United States. A wounded son of an Episcopalian family in Washington, DC, was listed by the War Department as missing, because the Nazis had failed to report him to the International Red Cross as captured. The soldier was convalescing in a hospital in Italy, where a Vatican official found him. A Baptist family in Kansas, as an expression of gratitude for news that their son was a war prisoner and not dead, sent the Holy Father their weekly tithe of

twenty-two dollars. Communicating with their families, the Vatican described details of injuries, deaths, internment, and photographs of the resting-place or turned over to the office of the American *chargé d'affaires* the belongings of soldiers. This was a sad, yet consoling work of mercy.

In view of the plight of the Jewish people of Europe, resolutions were adopted at the January 1939 meeting of the Jewish Congress in Geneva. Dr. Nahum Goldmann, chairman, stated: "We record the Jewish people's deep appreciation of the stand taken by the Vatican against the advance of resurgent paganism which challenges all traditional values of religion as well as inalienable human rights upon which alone enduring civilization can be found. The Congress salutes the Supreme Pontiff, symbol of the spiritual forces which under many names are fighting for the re-establishment of the rule of moral law in human society."[6]

On September 1, 1939, Nazi tanks crossed the Polish border. This was the beginning of World War II. In his encyclical, *Summi Pontificatus* (October 27, 1939), Pius XII condemned Hitler's actions. On December 28, 1939, the Pope paid a ceremonial call on King Victor Emmanuel III and Queen Elena at the Quirinal Palace. The visit was to return that made by the King and Queen a week earlier, and also to demonstrate the Vatican's support of Italy's neutrality.

The King and Queen of Italy visit the Pope in the Vatican.

The Pope returns the visit on December 28, 1939.

Historical records show that Pius XII acted as a link to the British government for a number of German dissidents desiring to overthrow Hitler. The Pope went beyond his usual caution, and maintained these contacts until the German invasion of Denmark and Norway in April 1940. The following month, when the Germans invaded the Low Countries, the Pope sent telegrams to the leaders of these besieged nations with his prayers for their deliverance. Soon after, Mussolini joined Hitler. When Nazis occupied Rome in September 1943, the Pope endeavored to save as many Jews as possible. He immediately issued directives to all convents and monasteries to open their doors to protect Jews. Meanwhile, Pope Pius XII invited Jews and other refugees to join the Vatican Palatine Guards. In a few months, their number increased from four hundred to four thousand.

Everywhere in Europe, persecuted people, the Jews especially, appealed to Pius XII. When some five hundred Jews embarked at Bratislava on a steamer for Palestine, their ship tried to enter the seaport of Istanbul, but was refused permission to land. Captured by an Italian patrol boat, the Jews were imprisoned in a camp at Rhodes. One of the prisoners managed to appeal to Pius XII for help. Thanks to the Pope's intervention, unknown to the Axis, the refugees were transferred to an improvised camp (Ferramonti-Tarsia) in Southern Italy, where they were found safe three years later, in December 1943.[7]

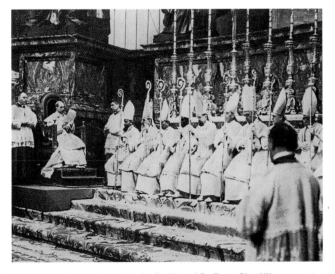

For his first papal ceremony in the Basilica of St. Peter, Pius XII consacrates twelve missionary bishops on October 29, 1939.

In an effort to avert World War II, Pius XII sends a radio-message on August 24, 1939. He pleaded: "Nothing is lost through peace; all can be lost through war."

CHAPTER V

Papal Audiences

After serving the Church under four Popes (Leo XIII, St. Pius X, Benedict XV and Pius XI) for almost two decades, on March 2, 1939 Eugenio Pacelli took the name of Pius XII and was entrusted with the keys of supreme jurisdiction given to the Prince of the Apostles: "Thou art Peter and upon this rock I will build My Church."

Viva il Papa! Viva il Papa! One can never forget the excitement and the resounding of these words during the papal audiences. The stimulation, the expectation are indescribable. During World War II, people crowded around Pius XII. He received hundreds of thousands of servicemen and women of every Allied nation. One audience inspired U.S. sailors to begin a rousing "Hip, hip, hooray—His Holiness!" Totally exhausted after the audiences, the Pope was always exhilarated by the expressions of love and

The Pope sends his blessing.

respect of thousands of his flock from every part of the world. The overwhelming enthusiasm reflects the almost universal esteem for Pius XII and the belief that the Pope is, in fact, the representative of Christ on earth.

The Pope always enjoyed receiving people of every nation and rank: statesmen and workers; writers and artists; the young and the old; the sick and the suffering; religious and lay men and women. Offering their gifts, young people opened their hearts and confided to him their cherished dreams. As a father with his children, he spoke to them according to their particular state, profession, work or condition.

Whether it was privately or in small or large groups, each person visiting His Holiness was truly a guest during a papal audience. No matter where one was staying in Rome, whenever invitations were requested, they were delivered by hand.

Everyone was his guest. Pope Pius XII called the audiences "windows on the world." This daily experience was kaleidoscopic and sometimes a source of confusion: pieces of clothing were lost, his hands bruised, and his pectoral cross broken. His movements were quick. One day he was not aware that his ring slipped off his hand. As a woman knelt earlier to kiss it, the ring remained in her hand. The elderly woman screamed that she had to see the Pope. The guards wanted to arrest her, but the Pope

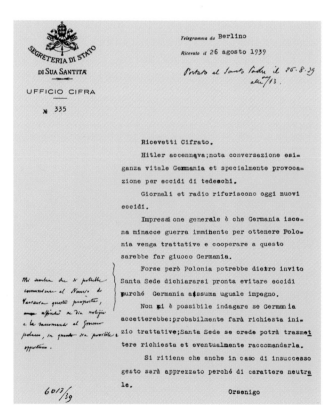

Transcript of Nunzio Orsenigo's telegram from Berlin dated August 26, 1939, suggesting that the Holy Father intervene between Poland and Germany, but warns that German intentions are unpredictable.

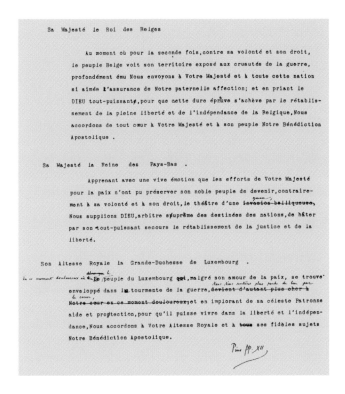

smilingly told her to approach him and then asked her to slip his Fisherman's ring back on.

Following Pius XII's meetings each morning with Vatican staff members, he had private or general audiences for people in all walks of life. Addressing each group, he reminded them of their duties and obligations and had extraordinary insight into all types of problems.

To bankers the Pope cautioned that money is not an end in itself, but merely an instrument to be used justly for securing the God-given rights of all men. To midwives he clarified the Church's continued stand against abortion and contraceptive practices. He recalled that this is not just Catholic teaching. It is rooted in the natural law, the rules of Creation as God made the world. He not only showed his appreciation of good craftsmanship as he spoke to jewelers but told streetcar conductors that he understood their vexations on the job. They knew he was trying to teach them the virtue of patience. To athletes he said that the important thing about sports is that it develops will power and Christian domination of the body, as well as "elevates the spirit above small-mindedness, dishonesty, and trickery."

Throughout his life Pacelli continued scholarly pursuits. In 1943, for example, in a discourse to the Pontifical Academy of Science, he forecast the development of atomic energy and discussed the disintegration which uranium undergoes when bombarded by neutrons. The Pope expressed the hope that its force would be harnessed for the service of man and not released for his destruction.

On September 19, 1945, the *New York Times* wrote: "Pope Pius XII this morning received Sir Alexander

On February 14, 1940, President Roosevelt acknowledged His Holiness' letter. Myron C. Taylor was the U.S. representative to the Vatican.

gy, urology, medico-moral problems, as well as accountancy and economics, moral guidance, statistics. Most of them were in French and Italian, but a few were in Spanish, German, English or Latin.

Vatican Protocol Ignored

Pius XII blended casualness with dignity and many times ignored Vatican protocol during the papal audiences. The story goes that, on some occasions, people filled with repentance would tremblingly ask to go to confession. Always a priest and aware of divine grace at work, the Holy Father never failed to step to a corner with the penitent sinner and grant him absolution, while others waited in awe.

In those days, women admitted to a papal audience had to wear long-sleeved, high-necked black dresses with a mantilla and a veil. A young woman newspaper correspondent during World War II was in a hurry, so her male companions smuggled her past guards to the great Consistorial Hall where the Pope would receive them. But when instructed to form a circle, the conspirators were forced to expose the young lady. As the guards were rushing her away, the Pope entered and signaled them to let her stay. He repaid her brashness with the gentle comment: "Ah, we see you are an American."

Screening for a general audience was not very intense. In fact, many ladies were not aware they had to dress according to protocol. One day, when asked to kneel, a young girl in culottes and wedgies and harlequin glasses refused. "I got a coat on—isn't that enough? I'm not a Catholic! Why should I kneel?" Everyone was embarrassed.

As the Pope arrived, the girl continued to abuse the guards. Suddenly the scene changed. The Pope approached her gently; she burst into tears on her knees. He comforted her and stretched forth his hands to raise her up, but she shook her head and begged his blessing. Pope Pius XII blessed her and the rest of the assemblage.

Compassion

Pius XII's love was manifested by his compassion. With thousands of people in larger audiences, the Pope had to move swiftly. One day, there was a

Fleming and discussed with him new uses of penicillin. The discoverer of penicillin presented the Pontiff a plate for cultivating mold to be used in research. Sir Alexander, after a twenty-minute audience, declared he was astonished at the Pope's knowledge of his discovery."

In 1951 Pius XII spoke on modern science and the proofs for the existence of God. On another occasion, he addressed the International Astronomical Union and spoke on the histopathology of the central nervous system. His speeches ranged from international penal law, toleration, psychiatry and clinical psychology, to medical genetics, opthamolo-

Pius XII and General George C. Marshall, U.S. Secretary of State, accompanied by his wife.

Draft letter of June 1, 1941 to Bishop von Preysing with Pius XII's corrections.

woman with a blind baby. He spoke consoling words to the woman while blessing her and the baby.

After moving away, Pius XII hesitated, and then turned back. The Pope took the baby in his arms, pressed it tenderly to his heart, carefully protecting the child against his large, pectoral cross. He spoke quietly to the mother. The woman was weeping. So was Pius XII.

Pius XII's love was evident in his smiling, affectionate gaze. All who came to the audiences were well aware of his warmth. Regardless of one's faith, people in all walks of life and of every religious denomination treasured a meeting with him.

One day an American actor and his wife were present. As the Pope entered the room, he approached the newly-weds. They recall that "there was electricity in the room when he blessed them." They wished him a happy birthday. His smile lit up the whole room. The Pope gave them medals they would always treasure. "But," said the American actor, "it is Pius XII's simplicity and holiness which will stay with us forever to remind us that it's easy to reach God. He is only a prayer away."

On another occasion, the chamberlain called a family of Americans who were waiting for an audience—father, mother and four children, the youngest in his mother's arms. When the baby began to cry, the mother pleaded with the chamberlain. He shook his head.

Young girls from different parts of the world present gifts to the Holy Father on his birthday.

Three young boys carrying flowers were met by a smiling Pope as he walked in his garden.

The mother saw a young woman and ran toward her. "Will you hold my baby for me?" she asked, and the surprised woman took him in her arms. However, soon the mother came hurrying back. "Thank you," she said. "Let me have my baby. His Holiness says he doesn't care if he cries. He wants to see him!"

The Soldier's Hat

Buried in the large group of faithful during a general audience a soldier shifted uneasily on his crutches. He could not kneel. Suddenly he saw Pius XII's compassionate eyes looking at him. Walking toward him, the Pope extended his hand. The soldier fumbled his hat from his right hand to his left in order to grasp the Pope's, and he dropped it. His Holiness bent down, grabbed the hat, placed it into the soldier's trembling hand and embraced him. The young man suddenly relaxed and smiled. As the Pope moved on, the soldier leaned on his crutches, held his hat aloft in triumph, and then joined the crowd shouting, *Viva il Papa! Viva il Papa!*

Saint Louis Cardinals

Pius XII loved sports. Athletes in every sport were warmly received. Far from causing them to be

timid in his presence, he would question them about their particular sport and manifest a vivid interest in the lastest developments. Speaking of sports, he would recall his visit to the USA during the 1936 World Series between the New York Yankees and the Giants.

During an audience, a group of American baseball players were amazed when Pius XII spoke about sports. One of them waited till the audience was almost over and, as the Pope turned away, he murmured, "I was a Cardinal once myself, Your Holiness." Immediately the Pope turned around: "And how could that have been, my son?" During the explanation, perplexed, Pius XII grinned. The baseball player treasures the Pope's reaction: "I guess I really walked into that one." Joe Medwick, of the Saint Louis Cardinals, could never figure out where he got the nerve to kid the Pope.

Three young boys present gifts to His Holiness on his birthday as he walks in the Vatican gardens.

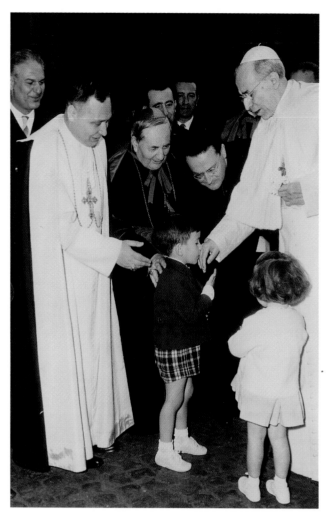

Movie Buff

People unfamiliar with Pius XII's character are amazed that the austere-looking pope was a movie buff. His favorite movie star was Clark Gable. When the movie King of Hollywood, his wife and daughter were granted a private audience, the subsequent callers were kept waiting in the reception hall for two hours. When Clark Gable's visit ended, Bishop Angelo Giuseppe Roncalli followed. This bishop is now known as Pope John XXIII.

Graham Greene

Several novels by Graham Greene had been banned by the Catholic Church. Nevertheless, Monsignor Giovanni Battista Montini recommended the theologically unorthodox writer to the Pope. At the time Pius XII was not very enthusiastic about Greene's novels. He told Father John Heenan (later Cardinal Archbishop of Westminster), "I think this man is in trouble. If ever he comes to you, you must listen."

Bloopers

An Anglican lady was invited to a special audience. She was alone and awaited the Pope in a small chamber. Now and then people dressed in the oddest fashions [e.g., the Swiss Guards in an outfit designed by Michelangelo and others in long robes] reassured her that the Pope would soon arrive. A tall, thin man wearing a white cassock chatted with her. She responded to his gentle questioning and they had a few polite laughs. At one point the Anglican lady whispered: "Confidentially, the main reason I want to see the Pope is because a lot of my Catholic friends gave me rosaries and medals and Lord knows what else for him to bless."

"We shall be happy to do so," said the man in white. The lady's jaw dropped. "Oh, no," she gulped. *"You're* the Pope!"

Laughter

In 1950, the Pope welcomed Olsen and Johnson to the Vatican. "Laughter has no religion," Pius XII wistfully emphasized, as he spoke about God's generosity with the gift of laughter. "There should be more of it in the world."

Among other celebrities from around the world who came to visit Pius XII were the Harlem Globetrotters when the Pope tapped his foot to "Sweet Georgia Brown." He also enjoyed a group of enthusiastic G.I.s who got carried away during an audience and sang, "For He's a Jolly Good Fellow."

A few days after the liberation of Rome, Lieutenant General Mark Clark, Commander of the Fifth Allied Army, paid his respects to the Pope: "I am afraid you have been disturbed by the noise of my tanks. I am sorry." Pius XII smiled and replied: "General, any time you come to liberate Rome, you can make just as much noise as you like."

Robert Murphy, U.S. Undersecretary of State, and Pius XII were among the diplomats in Germany during the mid-1920s. When they met after the war, Murphy reminisced about how they had underestimated Hitler. Both had reported to their governments that he would never come to power. In response to Murphy, the Pope smiled and said, "In those days, you see, I was not infallible."

64

A young girl offers bread to the Holy Father.

Italian Journalist

Leo Longanesi, a renowned Italian journalist and publisher, was indignant over the anticlerical campaigns against the Church. One day he suggested to the Pope that a particular day be designated when all Italian newspapers in Italy would print the full story about the charitable works of the Church during World War II. Pius XII responded: "Only God must be testimony to what is done for our neighbor!"

Although Pius XII would not publicize his own good deeds, others have. It suffices to mention a recent story which is part of the official Italian war record (*International Herald Tribune*, October 22, 2001). This information is one of the many examples of Pius XII's actions on behalf of Jewish refugees.

From 1943 to 1945, Leonardo Marinelli was a commander in the Royal Finance Guard in the Aprica internment camp, located in northern Italy. His *Diary* records an entry for September 12, 1943. The Pope sent Giuseppe Carozzi, a young Italian priest to Marinelli requesting that 300 Jewish Yugoslav internees be given permits to Switzerland. Despite strict Nazi orders forbidding Jews, prison-

ers of war, or anyone who had not joined Mussolini's northern Italian puppet Republic of Salò from crossing the border, Marinelli complied with the Pope's wishes. During the next four days as the group crossed the border, guards were seen "carrying bags for some of the fugitives."

Later, Marinelli himself was placed in an internment camp by the Nazis. He escaped. In his testimony to the Finance Guard high command in July 1945, Marinelli confirmed what he had written in his *Diary*.

The Pope's "zucchetto"

It is impossible to forget the moving experience of being with Pope Pius XII. His character combined all the merits of the papal office. All present breathe an atmosphere that could arise in no other place. His words make a deep impression on everyone.

Pius XII's personal magnetism, his warmth and affection, his compassion and love are characteristics that inspire everyone who has had the privilege of being in his presence. Each person was regarded as his personal guest. Though burdened with the

His Holiness congratulates Gino Bartoli, champion of the 1948 Tour de France.

cares of the world, Pius XII listened attentively to all who approached him. He radiated sanctity and peace; his dark luminous eyes looked at everyone with paternal affection. Whenever someone requested his "zucchetto," he would willingly give it. I have one in my possession. Indeed, I re-live those precious moments when, during the *baciamano* in Saint Peter's Basilica his niece, Elena Rossignani Pacelli, introduced me to him in 1957.

Pius XII knew so much about all the professions that one is astonished at his ability to speak so clearly and effectively in so many languages. In April 1954, he addressed a group of English doctors: "How exalted, how worthy of all honour is the character of your profession! The doctor has been appointed by God Himself (cf. Eccl. 38,1) to minister to the needs of suffering humanity. He who created that fever-consumed or mangled frame, now in your hands, who loves it with an eternal love, confides to you the ennobling charge of restoring it to health. You will bring to the sick-room and the operating table something of the charity of God, of the love and tenderness of Christ, the Master Physician of soul and body. That the blessing of the King of

Kings may descend upon you and your work and all your dear ones and your beloved country and remain forever, is the wish and prayer that rise from Our affectionate heart."

The Pope's Apartment

Each day a bus from a Minor Seminary in Rome arrived at St. Peter's Basilica bringing young boys wearing red cassocks and white surplices to serve the private Masses of visiting priests from all parts of the world. They were entrusted with a special kit with unconsecrated hosts and wine. Between Masses they would walk in and out of rooms to see if their services were needed. One day two fourteen-year-old seminarians were in this group.

Having made a wrong turn, they were in a labyrinth of halls and beautifully decorated rooms. At that early hour they did not encounter many people. Those who passed by, smiled, but did not question them. After all, they were dressed as altar boys and everyone assumed they knew where to go. They roamed around in a leisurely manner, not only intrigued but truly fascinated by the splendor.

However, the young seminarians were frightened when they realized they were lost. They panicked as they rushed in and out of rooms and corridors. Finally they reached a small library. As they entered, a kind-looking priest in a white cassock asked if he could help them. They explained they were on their way to serve Mass and were lost. Taking them by the hand, he told them not to worry. He invited them to a room in an adjoining apartment where he served them cookies and milk. While the boys enjoyed the treat, the priest spoke to them in a friendly manner. He then said: "Now the Holy Father gives you and your family a special blessing." The boys, shocked to learn they were with the Pope, knelt down for the blessing.

As they chatted, the Pope then directed them to St. Peter's Square. He advised them to go to the bus. Thrilled with this extraordinary experience, the boys, upon returning to the Seminary, related every detail of their encounter with the Pope. The altar boys had been lost, but they found His Holiness, Pope Pius XII. One of the boys later became a priest. His name is Father Joseph Rinaldo.

Minister of Peace

Pius XII reaffirmed the rights of the family, the rights of parents to supervise their children's education, and the rights of conscience, stressing the fundamental unity of all mankind under the fatherhood of God.

When there was danger that Rome would be involved in serious fighting between the Allied and German troops, the Pope went to the Church of Saint Ignatius Loyola. He remained on his knees throughout the night, praying before the sacred image of the Madonna del Divino Amore. Joining the Pontiff as he prayed for peace were the clergy and faithful of Rome. The city of Rome was saved!

Pius XII was a minister of peace in a warring world. When he was told that Stalin inquired about the number of divisions in his army, he said: "You may tell my son Joseph he will meet my divisions in heaven." That was Pacelli's secret. Even of Stalin he could say "my son." And mean it. He spoke many languages, but the only language that inspired others, was the language of his heart.

The Wisdom of Pius XII

Wisdom, guided by faith, is the core of all human formation. It is a power that enlightens consciences, frees them from all servitude and renders them capable of good. During the Second Vatican Council, Pius XII was quoted more than any other writer except the Sacred Scriptures. His words served the Council Fathers and show the breadth of his theology and his understanding of the needs of the Church in the twentieth century.

For nearly two decades, in simple yet loving statements, Pope Pius XII addressed words of wisdom to the faithful. Among his papal teachings, for example, it is interesting to note the unprecedented official Catholic pronouncements on the subject of womanhood. On October 21, 1945, Pius XII called for Catholic women to enter public life: "She must compete with man for the good of civic life, in which she is, in dignity, equal to him." Pius XII's treasured words continue to inspire the faithful:

The Aged: "People are inclined to reprove the elderly for what they no longer do, instead of reminding them of what they have done and recognize the wisdom of their judgments."

Art: "Art helps men, notwithstanding all the differences of character, education and civilization ... to pool their respective resources in order to complement one another."

Conscience: "Christian morality must be taught to our youth and inculcated in the youthful consciences by those who, in the family or in the school, have the obligation to attend to their education."

Education: "It is never too early to mold the character and habits of a child. Education begins at the cradle; and the first school, which nothing can replace, is that of the domestic hearth."

Family: "In the order of nature, among social institutions there is none that is dearer to the Church than the family. … Parents must give their children a wealth of faith and the atmosphere of hope and charity."

Harmony: "If three notes are sufficient to fix with their harmony the tonality of a musical composition, the song of spring could be condensed into three notes, the harmony of which brings his soul in tune with God Himself: faith, hope and charity."

Humanism: "Ideas, good or bad, guide the world. Some philosophers aim their views at projecting a ray of light on present day questions; others disturb the winds and sow confusion, particularly among the fine intellectual youth who tomorrow will be called to guide the coming generation."

Love: "God's masterpiece is man, and to this masterpiece of love, He has given a power to love unknown to irrational creatures: personal, conscious, free; that is to say, subject to the control of his responsible will."

Matrimony: "In the life of a wedded couple an essential nourishment of happiness is their mutual trust in sharing thoughts, aspirations, worries, joys and sorrows."

Peace: "Nothing is lost with peace; all can be lost with war. Let men come again to understand one another. Negotiating with good will and with respect for their reciprocal rights, they will perceive that honorable success is never precluded to sincere and constructive negotiations."

Prayer: "One finds God in prayer. He is a kind Father who will open to you His arms and heart. If you are in a state of grace, you will see in the intimacy of your soul with the eyes of faith God ever present."

Progress: "It is a clear principle of wisdom that every progress is truly such if it knows how to add new conquests to the old; if it knows how to store up experience."

Reason and Faith: "The homage which reason renders faith does not humiliate reason but honors it and exalts it, for the highest achievement of the progress of human civilization is that it facilitates the path of faith as it evangelizes the world."

Science: "If it is the duty of science to look for coherence and draw inspiration from sound philosophy, the latter may not arrogate to itself the claim to determine truths which belong exclusively to the sphere of experience and scientific method."

The State: "The more conscientiously the competent authorities of the State respect the rights of the minority, the more surely and effectively can it demand of its members that they carry out loyally the civic duties which are shared with other citizens."

Womanhood: "In virtue of a common destiny here on earth, … there is no field of human activity that must remain closed to women. Her horizons reach out to the regions of politics, work, the arts, sports— but always in subordination to the primary functions fixed by nature itself."

War on War: "If ever a generation had to feel deep down in its conscience the cry "War on war!" it is certainly the present one. … It has lived war's unspeakable atrocities so intensely that the recollection of so many horrors cannot but remain impressed in its memory and in the depths of its soul."

Vatican Storehouse

Vatican relief efforts—clothes, food, medicine, books—for the suffering throughout the world stemmed from Pius XII. The ceasing of hostilities did not end the sufferings of homeless survivors. At Villa Walsh, Morristown, New Jersey, Mother Ninetta Jonata, started a campaign in support of Pius XII's efforts and helped relieve the terrible destruction, hunger, sickness, and death caused by the brutal conflict. Countless cases of food, clothing, medicine, and other necessities were prepared at Villa Walsh and sent to the Pope for the relief of destitute war victims. The last shipload arrived in Naples on the *Michelangelo* (June 3, 1966), and was brought to the Vatican storehouse for distribution to the needy. It arrived on the Vatican railway (the world's shortest). The marble station, less than one-fifth of a mile of track from warehouse to outer wall, connected with the Italian state railroad. The Vatican enjoyed a freight discount of more than half on any shipment that entered the walls. Materials for mission and relief work were then transferred to a needy world.

A letter from the Secretary of State, dated June 18, 1947, refers to cases of supplies that had arrived within a few months from America: "29 cases on the ship, *City of Athens*; 60 cases on the *Exiria*; 90 cases on the *Waimea*." This letter included a request for soccer balls to help children adjust in the aftermath of the war. In his own hand the Pope wrote: "Your generous charity, beloved daughter, towards the suffering poor of Italy has been brought to Our attention. It has helped Us to widen the field of Our benefactions...December 31, 1949, Pius PP. XII."

Pius XII took special care of Vatican personnel. Only Vatican City residents could buy at its supermarket at one-half the cost outside. The farm at Castelgandolfo supplied much of the produce, eggs, cheese, and milk. During World War II there were four hundred New Hampshire chickens for eggs, and nearly fifty Frisian cows for milk. Much of what the farm provided was sent free to a hospital in Rome.

Vox Populi, Vox Dei!

Pius XII was the "Good Shepherd." He took care of his flock and remained in Rome during World War II. When Jews and other refugees were hidden in the Vatican, he provided for their needs. Whenever possible, Kosher foods for the Jews were supplied. Because everyone else could not have heat during the winter months, he refused to have heat in his apartment. He would not accept coffee during the war when he could not serve it to his "guests." He took care of his flock and remained in Rome during the war to assist them.

In 1943, as millions of Jews and other Europeans suffered the horrors of the Holocaust, the eternal city was bombed. The Holy Father hurried from the Vatican to the streets of Rome. He stood in the midst of terrorized people as buildings collapsed in piles of smoldering rubble. The Romans ran toward him for guidance and strength. With hands and white cassock smeared with the blood of the dead and the wounded, Pius XII blessed and consoled his flock. While civil authorities fled, the Pontiff personally took care of the immediate needs of the victims, providing food and distributing funds to the homeless.

Several years later, when an artist presented the Pope's portrait, His Holiness wrote beneath it in his own hand: "We pray that Almighty God may have mercy on this stricken world, and cause misunderstanding and hatred to cease, truth and charity to prevail, and that under His guiding Spirit the nations may soon enjoy the blessings of a lasting peace. From the Vatican, January 25, 1948 Pius PP. XII."

Pope Pius XII was the "Good Shepherd," selflessly dedicated to the Church, and to the glory of God. Contrary to how posterity has portrayed him, he was truly interested in the lives of approximately 450,000,000 members of his flock and in all members of the human race.

The Romans gave him the title, *Defensor Civitatis*; his contemporaries throughout the world acclaimed him, *Pastor Angelicus*. Indeed, the voice of the people is the voice of God. *Vox populi, Vox Dei!*

CHAPTER VI

Campaign of Vilification

The Catholic Church did not surrender into silence and numerous protests and interventions were made through the nuncios and ambassadors. In his book, *The Vatican and Its Role in World Affairs* (p. 147), Charles Pichon explained that the Nazis were hostile to Catholics and Jews. He testified that Pius XII's speeches on behalf of victims of Nazi terrorism were clear: "The pontifical texts condemned most strongly the antisemitic persecutions, the oppression of invaded lands, the inhuman conduct of the war, and also the deification of earthly things which were made into idols: the Land and the Race, the State and the Class. In the positive order, these documents urged the Christian restoration of family life and education, the harmonious reconstruction of society, the admittance of the working man to common and private property, the equality of nations, small and large,

Minister von Ribbentrop meets with Pius XII on March 11, 1940. The Pope spoke about the horrors of the war and recommended peace with justice.

Refugees sleep in the reception hall at Castelgandolfo.

November 5, 1943: the papal apartment at Castelgandolfo is bombed.

Vatican City State motor vehicles used to distribute food to refugees in Rome.

ly represent the Vatican defense of the Jews with the German Government and to alert the Nazis about the dangers of antisemitic politics."

Truth and justice demand a re-evaluation of the attacks against Pius XII, claiming "silence," "moral culpability," or "anti-Semitism." The long, anti-Catholic essay based on Daniel Jonah Goldhagen's controversial new book, *A Moral Reckoning: the Catholic Church during the Holocaust and Today* in the January 21, 2002 issue of *The New Republic*, is inaccurate and misleading. The *Osservatore Romano* condemned Adolf Hitler, Nazism, racism and anti-Semitism by name. Cardinal Secretary of State Pacelli's efforts to prevent World War II and the Holocaust have been ignored. His messages on

the participation of impoverished peoples in the natural resources of the globe, the suppression of hate propaganda and an international organization for disarmament and the maintenance of peace."

When Adolf Hitler was nominated Chancellor of Germany on January 30, 1933, the first official step taken by the Vatican Secretary of State, Cardinal Eugenio Pacelli, who six years later would become Pope Pius XII, was to defend the Jews. Robert Leiber, SJ, clearly demonstrates that the Holy See informed the Apostolic Nunzio in Berlin to "official-

The Pope visits the Vatican bakery before distribution of bread to wartime victims.

Vatican trucks prepare for distribution of food to refugees in Rome.

British prisoners of war protected by the Vatican.

Russian prisoners of war in Italy.

Russian prisoners of war attend papal audience.

Pius XII delivers his 1941 Christmas message.

Pius XII meets with wounded war victims.

Jewish tributes, the hundreds of pages of sworn depositions—all are dismissed by his accusers.

Throughout his papacy, Pope Pius XII was almost universally regarded as a saintly man, a scholar, a man of peace, a tower of strength, and a compassionate defender and protector of all victims of the war and genocide that had drenched Europe in blood. At the end of the war Western nations paid tribute to his efforts on behalf of the oppressed. When Pius XII died, Jews praised him for his help and were among the first to express sorrow and gratitude for his solicitude during the Holocaust.

Documentary evidence and the testimony of his contemporaries prove that Pius XII was a committed defender and protector of the victims of war and hatred which drenched Europe in blood. Pius XII ordered the Congregation of the Holy Office to issue a formal and explicit condemnation of the mass

Vatican Radio, his participation in the plot of German generals to overthrow Hitler, the testimony of countless witnesses, Eichmann's diaries, the Pope's intervention for Lend-Lease to Russia, the evidence produced at Nuremberg, the extraordinary

Andreotti and Storchi, president of the ACLI, with His Holiness. (right) Monsignor Venini; (left) Monsignor Dante.

76

An article in a Geneva newspaper (September 8, 1942) tells how Pius XII protested the treatment of Jews in Vichy France. The Pétain government had instructed local church authorities to ignore the papal protest. Nevertheless it was read in most churches.

murder going on in Germany in the name of improving the race. The decree was published on December 6, 1940, in *L'Osservatore Romano*. At the end of World War II, Western nations paid tribute to Pius XII's efforts on behalf of the oppressed. When he died in 1958, the Jewish communities of Europe praised him for his help and expressed sorrow and gratitude for his solicitude during the Holocaust. In the 1960s, there began a campaign of vilification against Pius XII. Today, his detractors continue to claim that he lacked courage, human compassion and a sense of moral rectitude. Hostile attacks by the media replace the historical record that showed him as a great leader.

This is the continuation of a smear campaign against the memory of Pius XII that began with Rolf Hochhuth's play, *The Deputy*, staged for the first time in 1963 in Germany. This "black legend,"

Vatican Bureau for research.

Dossiers, letters, related documents of war prisoners.

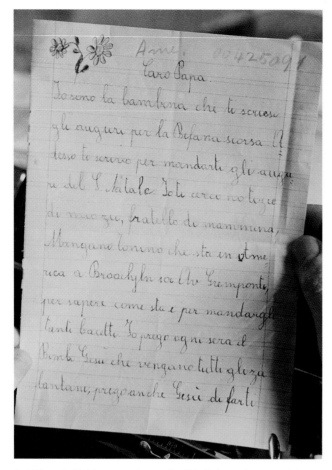

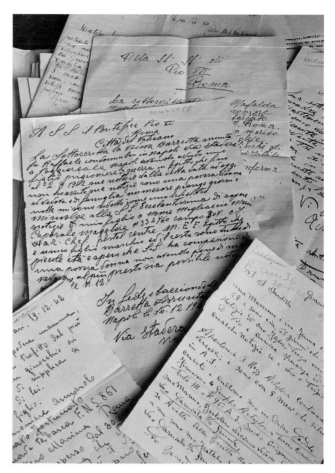

A child sends Christmas greetings to the Holy Father and requests information on her uncle, a prisoner of war in Brooklyn, New York.

The Vatican responded to hundreds of thousands of requests for information about prisoners of war.

Requests for information were received from every country in the world.

July 19, 1943: Pope Pius XII addressing the crowd after the bombing of Rome.

accusing the Pope of refusing to speak out about the Holocaust in spite of his detailed knowledge of Jewish suffering, was devoid of any factual basis.

It is claimed that, during the war, either due to political calculation or faintheartedness, Pius XII remained unmoved and silent before the crimes against humanity that his intervention would have prevented. In view of the neutrality of the Vatican, how could he have intervened?

If the Pope had openly condemned the Nazis, he would have also had to openly condemn the Fascists and the Communists. He was a prisoner of the Germans and of the Italians. Nazi and Fascist intelligence organizations invaded the Vatican. Important services were entirely controlled by the Italian government: food, water, electricity, sewage. Communication was censored: mail, telephone, and telegraph.

The Allies wanted Pius XII to condemn the Nazis, but they did not want him to criticize the Communists. Pius XII could not violate neutrality. Nor could he make partial public condemnations. Nonetheless, the Pope's voice was heard on the Vatican Radio and through *L'Osservatore Romano*.

The Record

Although the world had not listened in 1939 to his pleas for peace and justice, the Pope tried to help alleviate the suffering of thousands of victims. In fact, when American bombers dropped tons of explosives on Rome, July 19, 1943, Pius XII comforted the injured, administered the Last Rites, and distributed money to those in need of food and clothing.

During the two-hour bombardment, buildings collapsed and bombs exploded on all sides. Constantly solicitous for the flock entrusted to him, the Pope hurried from the Vatican to the damaged Basilica of Saint Lawrence Outside the Walls. The people of Rome regarded him as a man of peace and a defender and protector of all victims of the war. Documents reveal Pius XII's constant, untiring steps and appeals on behalf of peace before and during the war. His efforts can only be characterized as extraordinary.

79

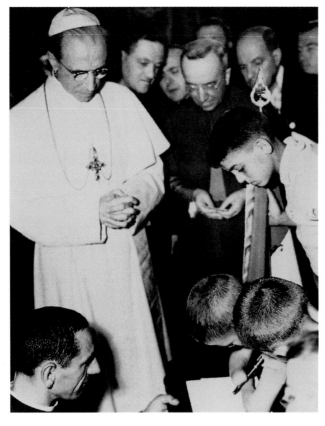

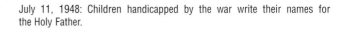
July 11, 1948: Children handicapped by the war write their names for the Holy Father.

Unfortunately, many critics cite evidence out-of-context. The record shows that the Catholic Church consistently assisted Jewish victims of Nazi anti-Semitism, even before the outbreak of World War II. Critics ignore documents describing the incomparable and unrelenting efforts of Pius XII, through his nuncios assisting as well, toward thousands of Jewish victims. In some instances, when confronted with frustration, Catholic appeals were made on behalf of Jews, baptized as Catholics, in the hope that they might be respected as such, or on the basis of their civil rights as specified in the concordats. These appeals should not detract from the singular efforts of the Catholic Church on behalf of all Jewish victims of the Nazis.

The persecution of the Catholic Church by the Nazis was evidenced by the incarceration of Priests, Sisters, and Brothers. Both Protestant and Catholic clergy in Holland sent a letter about the treatment of Jews and other minorities to Arthur Seyss-Inquart, the Reich Commissar, who then threatened that, unless they were silent, he would round up baptized Jews. Catholic bishops refused to obey and, on July 26, 1942, sent a pastoral letter that was read from all Catholic pulpits in the Netherlands.

The National Socialist Mayor of Rotterdam responded: "When the terrorism of the Church

widens its scope and calls for sabotage, as it did in these letters, the time has come for the party to react in an appropriate manner."[7] Consequently, Jewish converts to Catholicism, including Edith Stein, were rounded up and sent to the concentration camps; Jewish converts to Protestantism were left unharmed.

Information appeared in the Milan newspaper *Il Giornale*, July 5, 1998, confirming what some historians have always believed: Hitler intended to kidnap the Pope. In fact, Hitler gave orders to occupy the Vatican. However, his plans did not materialize.

Gratitude of Jewish Community

On December 1, 1944 the *New York Times* reported that the World Jewish Congress publicly thanked the Holy See for its protection of Jews, especially in Hungary; in October 1945, the World Jewish Congress made a financial gift to the Vatican in recognition of the Vatican's work to save the Jews; in May 1955, the Israeli Philharmonic gave a command performance of Beethoven's Seventh Symphony at the Vatican as a gesture of thanks to the Pope for his services to Jews during the war. Delighted with the magnificent performance, the Pontiff was photographed in the midst of the Israeli Orchestra, gave his blessing and afterwards granted an audience to the musicians.

In contrast to the esteem Pius XII enjoyed until his death in 1958, his reputation today suffers many unjust attacks. Some say that a theological condemnation of the Holocaust would have made a difference. Others want to weaken the moral authority of the papacy. However, according to Michael Novak, these critics "are deflecting attention from themselves. …Today's charges against Pope Pius XII cannot stand scrutiny."[9]

What Pius XII did for the Jews directly and indirectly through his diplomatic representatives and the bishops is well documented. At the end of World War II, Dr. Joseph Nathan, representing the Hebrew Commission, addressed the Jewish community, expressing heartfelt gratitude to those who protected and saved Jews during the Nazi-Fascist persecutions. "Above all," he stated, "we acknowledge the Supreme Pontiff and the religious men and women

80

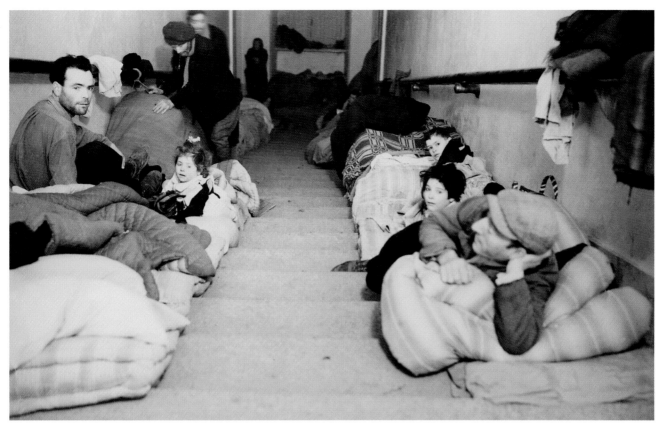

Homeless and refugees in makeshift dormitories at Castegandolfo.

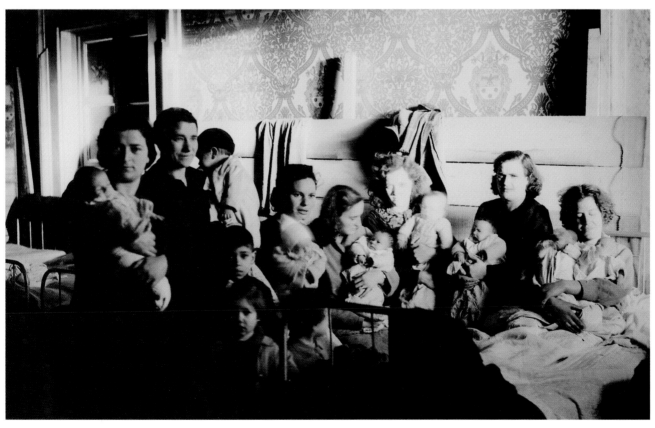

Refugees, mostly women and children, make a home in the papal apartments at Castelgandolfo.

VATICANO is clearly visible on the flank of a lorry assigned to the transportation of refugees.

who, executing the directives of the Holy Father, recognized the persecuted as their brothers and, with great abnegation, hastened to help them, disregarding the terrible dangers to which they were exposed."

Reuben Resnick, American Director of the Committee to Help Jews in Italy, declared that "all the members of the Catholic hierarchy in Italy, from Cardinals to Priests, saved the lives of thousands of Jews, men, women, and children who were hosted and hidden in convents, churches, and other religious institutions."[10]

Chief Rabbi Alexander Safran, of Bucharest, Rumania, made the following statement on April 7, 1944, to Nuncio Andrea Cassulo, Papal Nuncio to Rumania: "In the most difficult hours which we Jews of Rumania have passed through, the generous assistance of the Holy See was decisive and salutary. It is not easy for us to find the right words to express the warmth and consolation we experience because of the concern of the Supreme Pontiff [Pius XII] who offered a large sum to relieve the sufferings of deported Jews—sufferings which had been pointed out to him by you after your visit to Transnistria. The Jews of Rumania will never forget these facts of historic importance."

The following petition was presented to Pope Pius XII in the summer of 1945 by twenty thousand Jewish refugees from Central Europe: "Allow us to ask the great honor of being able to thank, personally, His Holiness for the generosity he has shown us when we were being persecuted during the terrible period of Nazi-Fascism."

There was a story in an American newspaper (January 1946) about a special Thanksgiving service in Rome's Jewish Temple that was heard over the radio. The Jewish chaplain of the Fifth American Army gave a discourse in which, among other things, he said: "If it had not been for the truly substantial assistance and the help given to Jews by the Vatican and by Rome's ecclesiastical authorities, hundreds of refugees and thousands of Jewish refugees would have undoubtedly perished before Rome was liberated."[11]

The Italian Jewish community on April 5, 1946, sent the following message to His Holiness, Pius XII: "The delegates of the Congress of the Italian Jewish Communities, held in Rome for the first time after the Liberation, feel that it is imperative to extend reverent homage to Your Holiness, and to express the most profound gratitude that animates all Jews for your fraternal humanity toward them

82

Dining halls instituted by the Vatican for homeless and refugees.

during the years of persecution when their lives were endangered by Nazi-Fascist barbarism. Many times priests suffered imprisonment and were sent to concentration camps and offered their lives to assist Jews in every way. This demonstration of goodness and charity that still animates the just, has served to lessen the shame and torture and sadness that afflicted millions of human beings. ...The Jews will perpetually remember how much, under the direction of the Pontiff, the Church did for them during that terrible period."

Israel Anton Zolli

Claims that Pope Pius XII never instructed religious to protect Jews during the war, are contradicted by the Chief Rabbi of Rome, Israel Anton Zolli.

Israel Zoller was born in Brodj, Galizia, on September 17, 1881. His family name was italianized to Zolli. They were Polish Jews and had been Rabbis for four centuries. In 1920 Israel was named Rabbi of Trieste which then belonged to the Austrian-Hungarian Empire. He also held the Hebrew Language and Literature Chair at the University of Padova. In 1940 he was deprived of this position by the Fascists and sent to Rome as Chief Rabbi.

The American Hebrew in New York published an interview with Rabbi Zolli on July 14, 1944. Having been hidden in the Vatican during the German occupation of Rome, he emphatically stated: "The Vatican has always helped the Jews and the Jews are very grateful for the charitable work of the Vatican, all done without distinction of race."

After the war, Rabbi Israel Zolli converted to Catholicism and wrote his memoirs, *Before the Dawn* (1954), claiming to have witnessed a vision of Christ, who called him to the faith. The voice he heard said: "You are here for the last time." It was Yom Kippur.

Zolli devoted an entire chapter in his memoirs to the German occupation of Rome and praised the Pope's leadership: "...The people of Rome loathed the Nazis and had intense pity for the Jews. They willingly assisted in the evacuation of the Jewish population into remote villages, where they were concealed and protected by Christian families. Christian families in the heart of Rome accepted Jews. There was money in the treasury for the support of destitute refugees thus hidden. The Holy Father sent by hand a letter to the bishops instruct-

The Vatican sends aid to the inhabitants of Montecassino.

ing them to lift the enclosure from convents and monasteries, so that they could become refuges for the Jews. I know of one convent where the Sisters slept in the basement, giving up their beds to Jewish refugees. In face of this charity, the fate of so many of the persecuted is especially tragic."

Rabbi Zolli is the most important non-Catholic witness to the role of Pius XII in wartime Italy dur-

ing the Nazi occupation and persecution of Jews. A biblical scholar whose courage and integrity cannot be challenged, Zolli was hidden in the Vatican. His wife and his twenty-year-old daughter Miriam were hidden in a convent. They were eye-witnesses of the deportation of Rome's Jews by the Gestapo in 1943.

Zolli asked to be received by the Pope. The meeting with Pius XII took place on July 25, 1944.

84

Nuns distribute food to the homeless.

Notes by Vatican Secretary of State Giovanni Battista Montini confirm the fact that on July 23 Rabbi Zolli addressed the Jewish Community in the Synagogue and publicly thanked the Holy Father for all he did to save the Jewish Community of Rome. His talk was transmitted by radio. On February 13, 1945, Rabbi Zolli was baptized by Rome's Auxiliary Bishop Luigi Traglia in the Church of Santa Maria degli Angeli. Present for the ceremony was Father Agostino Bea, the Pope's confessor and future protagonist during the Council with regard to the dialog between religions. In gratitude to Pius XII, Israel Zolli took the name, Eugenio. A year later his wife and daughter were also baptized.

Miriam recalls the prophetic words of her father about Pope Pius XII: "You will see, they will blame Pope Pius XII for the world's silence in the face of the Nazis' crimes!" She insists that her father never abandoned his Judaism: "He felt he was a Jew who had come to believe in the Jewish Messiah."

In his book, *Antisemitismo*, Rabbi Zolli states: "World Jewry owes a great debt of gratitude to Pius XII for his repeated and pressing appeals for justice on behalf of the Jews and, when these did not prevail, for his strong protests against evil laws and procedures."

Zolli, who found shelter in the Vatican during the war stated: "No hero in all of history was more militant, more fought against, none more heroic than Pius XII in pursuing the work of true charity! ...and this on behalf of all the suffering children of God."

Sister Pascalina Lehnert

Implementing the Pope's charitable works as Nuncio, Cardinal Secretary of State and Supreme Pontiff was Sister Pascalina Lehnert. She was born August 29, 1894 and became a member of the Teaching Sisters of the Holy Cross.

Pius XII was a humble person who did not want his many good works and accomplishments revealed. Sister Pascalina, his housekeeper from 1923-1958—the period when he was Nuncio in Germany to his death—served him faithfully, respecting his wishes even after his death when writing her own memoirs where she records his words about Hitler.

Leone Bondi and Virginia Piperno with three of their six children. The entire family of eight was deported to Auschwitz, where they all perished.

One day, Pius XII prepared an official protest to be published the following day in the *Osservatore Romano*. As he entered the kitchen and stood before the blazing fireplace, he told Sister Pascalina that he decided not to have his protest printed and would now burn it. She objected and reminded him that it might be useful in the future. Pius XII said: "This protest is stronger than that of the Dutch bishops. I thought about filing it but, if the Nazis come and find it, what will happen to the Catholics and Jews in Germany? No, it is better to destroy this strong protest." With that, he threw it into the fire. Instead, he ordered Amleto Cicognani, Apostolic Delegate in Washington, DC, to have the text of the Dutch bishops' protest published and circulated in the United States.

According to Giorgio Angelozzi-Gariboldi's book, *Pius XII, Hitler and Mussolini* (1988), when the Germans were planning to invade the Vatican and kidnap the Pope in 1943, arrangements for a safe haven were developed. Attorney Milo di Villagrazia, Monsignor Edoardo Prettner Cippico of the Secretariate of State and the architect of the Apostolic Palaces, Count Enrico Galeazzi met secretly with Sister Pascalina. Plans were that the Pope would be clandestinely transferred to Galeazzi's villa, about 120 kilometers from the Vatican. Soon after, he would be accompanied to safety in Spain. There General Francisco Franco Bahamonde would be honored to host the Pope and remove him from the fury of the Nazis.

The villa was well situated on the sea and, except with a very small vehicle, it was very difficult to reach. When Sister Pascalina inspected the house, she climbed a wall and slipped, breaking her ankle. This did not deter her from continuing her task nor did it discourage her. She decided that the villa could be adapted to the needs of the Pontiff. Little did she realize that the Pope would adamantly refuse to leave the Vatican!

Among the 900 pages of depositions for the beatification of Pius XII, Sister Pascalina clearly states (*Processo Romano*, pp. 84-85): "Pius XII did not issue a condemnation of Nazism because the German and Austrian bishops dissuaded him from making additional protests that would undoubtedly irritate Hitler. Jews and Christians had suffered in the past because of Vatican pronouncements and they feared increased retaliation. The Pope not only opened the doors of the Vatican to protect the persecuted, but he encouraged convents and monasteries to offer hospitality. The Vatican provided provisions for these people. The accusation that Pius XII was indifferent to the needs of the victims is without foundation. He ordered me to spend his inheritance and personal funds to provide for those who wished to leave Italy and go to Canada, Brazil or elsewhere. Note that $800 were needed for each person who emigrated. Many times the Pope would ask me to deliver a sealed envelope, containing $1,000 or more, to Jewish families (Session CLXIII, March 17, 1972)."

In general, while begging for help, the Jews who were in contact with Pope Pius XII insisted that he avoid any public action.

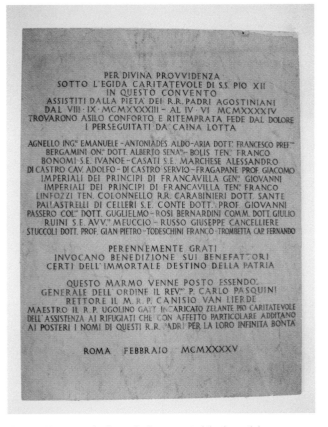

Plaque with names of refugees in the convent of the Augustinians.

CHAPTER VII

Documents of the Holy See

Indeed, historians must base the written history of events on documents, and not only on testimonies. But there are rules: documents that concern people still alive or which, once revealed, could hinder negotiations in process cannot be published. This criteria was followed in the publication of the Holy See's documents.

Did Pius XII give instructions during the Holocaust? Yes, he did. Is documentation available to confirm this statement? Yes, countless documents exist. One need only consult the eleven volumes (Vol. III is in two tomes) of Vatican documents.

To provide this documentation, Pope Paul VI in 1963 ordered the opening of the Vatican archives. He selected Jesuit Church historians: Pierre Blet, Angelo Martini, Burkhart Schneider, and Robert A. Graham. Their combined scholarship produced *Actes et Documents du Saint Siège relatifs à la Seconde Guerre Mondiale*, published between 1965 and 1981 by Città del Vaticano. Historian Eamon Duffy stated that the *Acts and Documents of the Holy See Relative to the Second World War*, "decisively established the falsehood of Hochhuth's specific allegations."

Historians may now study the role and activity of the Holy See during the war. The documents show the groundlessness of the attacks on Pius XII regarding his so-called "silence," and establish once and for all times the action of the Holy See in sympathy with the victims of the war and in opposition especially to the racial persecutions.

During the winter of 1965, Father Robert Leiber, who had been for more than thirty years the private assistent of Eugenio Pacelli, disclosed the existence of drafts of the letters of Pius XII to the German bishops. These personal letters best explain the Pope's instructions. They show objectively the true attitude and behavior of Pius XII during the conflict and, consequently, the groundlessness of the accusations against his memory.

There is no evidence that the attitude Pacelli is said to have absorbed during his years as Nuncio to that country was in any way favorable to the Hitler Government. Of forty-four major addresses in Germany, forty condemned some aspect of Nazism.

A page from the diary of the Religious Teachers Filippini, Via delle Botteghe Oscure, Rome.

Pacelli comforted the Catholic Church in Germany which was being persecuted by the German government. His efforts—joining President Roosevelt to keep Italy out of the conflict; sending the May 10, 1940 telegrams to the sovereigns of Belgium, Holland, and Luxemburg after the invasion by the *Wehrmacht*; courageously advising Mussolini and King Vittorio Emanuele III to explore a separate peace—surely do not suggest such a pro-Nazi attitude.

Neither does the accusation of "silence" hold up. What appears to be silence was, in fact, a concealment of action conducted through the nunciatures

LE RABBIN Andre Z A O U I
****
Aumonier Capitaine
Du Corps Expeditionnaire Francais
****

Secteur Postal, 70.024, le 22 Juin 1944.-

A Sa Saintete Pie XII, Chef de la

Chretiente

****

Que votre Saintete daigne me permettre de me rappeler a son bon souvenir. Je suis le rabbin de l'Armee Francaise venu vous voir a l'audience publique que votre Saintete a bien voulu accorder aux tres nombreux officiers et soldats allies, le mardi 6 Juin 1944 a 12 h 20. Je rends graces a l'Eternel de m'avoir accorde de voir ce jour ou je pus dire au Chef de l'Eglise les sentiments de profonde reconnaissance et de tres respectueuse admiration, de mes freres Israelites du Corps Expeditionnaire - Francais, pour le bien immense et la charite incomparables que votre Saintete a prodigues aux Juifs d'ITALIE, notamment aux enfants, femmes et veillards de la Communaute de ROME.

Il m'a ete donne de visiter l'ISTITUTO PIO XI qui a protege durant plusde six mois une soixantaine d'enfants juifs dont quelques petits refugies de France.- J'ai ete tres emu de la sollicitude paternelle que tous les maitres apportaient a ces jeunes ames : " nous n'avons fait que notre devoir" me dit simplement le preffeto.-

Quelle ne fut pas encore mon emotion lors de l'office religieux du jeudi 8 Juin qui consacra la reouverture de la synagogue de ROME, fermee par les Allemands depuis Octobre dernier.- Un pretre francais, evade de France, qui rendit lui aussi d'inoubliables srvices a de nombreuse familles juives de ROME, et qui etait present a la synagogue, le R.P. - BENOIT, fut acclame par la foule des fideles a qui il dbit des paroles de sympathie qui toucherent profondement ces ames encore endolories. "J'aime les Juifs de tout mon coeur, dit-il, entre autre". Comme ces mots resonnerent dans ma memoire. Ils me rappelerent ceux que S.S. PIE XI dit a la Chretiente : " Nous sommes spirituellement des semites".-

Quelle magnifique manifestation de fraternite, si grande dans sa simplicite intime. Israel ne l'oubliera pas. Coute que coute, il continuera d'accomplir sa mission, en pratiquant et en enseignant sa Loi d'Amour de Dieu et du prochain. Je suis pour ma part un de ces nombreux - fils d'Israel qui, dans les moments les plus penibles des dix dernieres annees, ont vu dans cette tragedie un signe de Dieu, et n'ont cesse de prier et d'agir pour que la foi revienne nous inspirer et eclaircir les hommes.-

Demain, les peuples seront appeles a s'entendre. J'ai la conviction que ce but ne sera atteint que si les responsables de toutes les collectivites humaines s'unissent pour preparer ensemble la Paix definitive fondee seulement sur les preceptes d'Amour contenu dans Le Livre.

A cet effet, j'ai l'insigne honneur de prier, votre - Saintete d'agreer l'essai ci-joint, de bien vouloir me faire connaitre son avis sur ce tres humble hommage d'un serviteur de Dieu, au Chef inconteste de l'Eglise.-

A. Zaoui

Rabbi André Zaoui informs the Holy Father of the assistance the Catholic Church gave to the Jews in France and to the French refugees in Rome.

YAD VASHEM יד ושם

The Holocaust Martyrs' and Heroes' Remembrance Authority רשות הזיכרון לשואה ולגבורה

Jerusalem, 17 October 1996

Ref: ANTONIOLI DON FRANCESCO - ITALY (7320)
ALESSANDRINI DON ARMANDO - ITALY (7320A)

We are pleased to announce that the above persons were awarded the title of "Righteous Among the Nations," for help rendered to Jewish persons during the period of the Holocaust.

A medal and certificate of honor will be mailed to the Israeli consulate/embassy listed below, which will organize a ceremony in their honor. Their names will also soon be added on the Righteous Honor Wall at Yad Vashem.

Copies of this letter are being mailed to the honorees, to persons who have submitted testimonies, and other interested parties.

Dr. Mordecai Paldiel
Director, Dept. for the Righteous

cc: ✓ Istituto Storico Salesiano - Via Della Pisana 1111, C.P. 9092, 00163 Roma - Italy
Mr. Guido Tagliacozzo - Peazzale G. Douhet 5, 00144 Roma
Mr. Anticoli Vittorio E. - Via A Cesari 26, 00152 Roma
Dr. Isacco Caviglia - Via Fonteiana 67, 00152 Roma
Mr. Fua Giorgio - Via Somalia 35, 00199 Roma
Mr. Di Castro Aldo - Via Ottorino Lazzarini 5, 00136 Roma
Mr. Rossi Maurizio Shlomo - Kibutz Rouhama 79180, D.N. Hof Ashkelon - Israel
Mr. Bice Migliau - Centro di Cultura Ebraica, Via Arco de'Tolomei 1, 00153 Roma
Ambassador Yehuda Millo, Embassy of Israel - Roma

1/M.P./D.W./

P.O.B. 3477, JERUSALEM 91034, FAX. 6433511 .פקס TEL. 6751611 .טל ,91034 ת.ד. 3477, ירושלים

Yad Vashem honors two Salesians: Father Francesco Antonioli and Father Armando Alessandrini.

British Ambassador Francis Osborne D'Arcy (left) and Monsignor Giovanni Battista Montini visit the homeless. These street children were called "Sciuscià."

and the bishops to avoid or, at least, limit the deportations and persecutions. In many speeches and in his letters to the German bishops, Pope Pius XII clearly explained that discretion was necessary. Documents show he constantly opposed the deportation of the Holocaust victims.

Father Pierre Blet, one of the four editors of the *Actes*, stated that "a public declaration would not have been of any help; it would have accomplished nothing except to aggravate the situation of the victims and multiply their number. ...Without Father Leiber, we would not have been aware of the existence of the drafts of Pius XII's letters to the German bishops and the collection would have been deprived of perhaps the most precious texts to understand the Pope's mind. But all of those texts taken together do not contradict at all what we learn from the diplomatic notes and correspondence."

In these documents we learn that Pius XII emphasized to the bishops the need to warn German Catholics against National Socialism as an enemy of the Church—a risky move on his part even more so in a time of war. This correspondence, published in the second volume of *Actes et Documents*, confirms the opposition of the Church to

National Socialism and the Church's compassion for the victims. Already there had been warnings— disseminated by Bishops Faulhaber and von Galen, and by many religious and clergymen in Germany—that culminated with the encyclical *Mit brennender Sorge*, read in all the German churches on Palm Sunday 1937.

Letters to the German Bishops

Volume II of the Vatican documents, *Actes et Documents du Saint Siège Relaltifs à la Seconde Guerre Mondiale 1965-1982*, is entitled *Lettres de Pie XII aux Évêques Allemands.*[12] Preceded by a sixty-page Introduction in French, there are 124 autographed letters written by Pope Pius XII and addressed to the German bishops during World War II. Of these, 103 are in German; the others in Latin.

These letters are not limited to a particular topic, nor do they constitute a systematic exposé. They treat of contemporary problems, about a particular situation. Clearly they reflect the current situation of the Church in Germany. The Pope gives counsel to his correspondents on the attitude they should adopt during their conflict with the regime; explains

June 1944: General De Gaulle visits Pius XII. He describes the visit in his memoirs.

the difficulties and the anguish of the Holy See; describes how he must safeguard its neutrality; offers reflections on what must be accomplished, or informs the Bishops of his efforts toward peace.

Attached to Letter 42 addressed to the Cardinal-Archbishop of Breslau, dated March 17, 1940, are two pages of Italian notes[13] used by Pius XII to bring to the attention of German Foreign Minister von Ribbentrop the actions committed against the Catholic Church in Germany.

These actions were contrary to the conditions of the Concordat. They included the suppression of Catholic schools, minor and major seminaries, religious houses, associations and charitable Catholic institutions and the elimination of every form of

religious education, substituting the catechism with the so-called National Socialist "Weltanschauung."

Pius XII reminded Ribbentrop that the Law of April 30, 1939 seriously violated the rights and the liberty of the Church itself. Sacrilegious vandalism was perpetrated, public manifestations against the Church were permitted, and religious functions, pastoral letters, pontifical documents were prohibited. Anti-Christian propaganda during conferences and in the media continued with arrests of ecclesiastics, censure of Church activities, calumnious and offensive attacks against the Catholic Church.

The Pontiff responded to the German bishops who, during their annual Episcopal Conference in Fulda, had sent him a report describing the terrible

General Eisenhower visits the Holy Father.

Archbishop Angelo Giuseppe Roncalli after an audience with Pius XII accompanied by Colonel Fixel and Major Mead, the American aviators who facilitated his trip from Istanbul to Paris where he presented his credentials to General De Gaulle on January 1, 1945.

A group of Jewish delegates from the concentration camps in Germany visit His Holiness.

An extract from Pius XII's discourse to the Jewish delegates in his own handwriting.

Nazi oppression. He thanked them for their attestation of strong faith and devotion and for informing him of the present sad conditions of the Church in Germany. Profoundly moved by their communication, the Pope reminded them that, throughout the centuries, persecutions were never lacking in the Church. He referred to the insidiousness of the situation and to their brave marytrdom:

"Thus the Catholic Church in Germany is oppressed by serious difficulties, as are clearly demonstrated by the many violences you mentioned: men, especially those who hold civic responsibilities, are forced to deny their Christian religion; limits are placed on your care for souls; young people are taught doctrines contrary to Christian dogma and are kept away from the clergy; almost all

Catholic newspapers and magazines have been suppressed; Religious Houses are gradually closed and their property confiscated. … While you are afflicted by these unjust dispositions, you are concerned about the greater ones that are feared imminent. You foresee indications of a turbulent tempest that will fall upon our beloved sons and daughters of Germany.

"You ask us, beloved sons and venerable brothers: 'What should be our defense? The arms of our adversary are numerous, the Church seems to be almost defenseless.' But then you immediately add: 'And yet, it is not permitted to despair' and you promise to be faithful to God and to Christ at any cost… You have expressed your resolutions with clarity and seriousness in your Pastoral Letter of last June 26, the

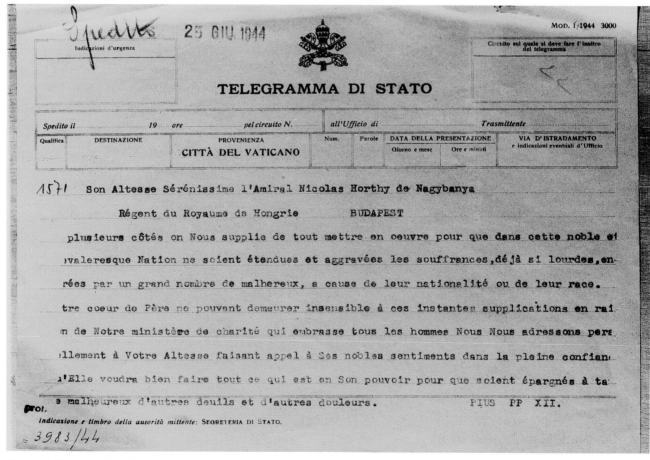

Telegram in French from Pius XII to Hungary's Regent, Niklos Horthy, protesting the deportation of Jews. The Pope pleaded with Horthy to use his office so that "many unfortunate people may be spared further afflictions and sorrows."

A child greets the Pope as he walks in the Vatican gardens.

reading of which moved me deeply… We do not doubt but that you will implement, unhesitatingly, with constancy and valor, the proposals you so courageously established. Your faith and that of your priests and faithful is worthy of admiration. May the indomitable fidelity that from the beginning of our pontificate has given us such comfort continue to shine in the midst of adversity…"

The letter concludes with hope in the future of the German Church and with the prayer that "the enemies of the Church may finally understand that there is nothing so wicked as hurting one's mother and, recognizing their errors, they will soon repent (Volume II, September 8, 1941)."

Message to the Cardinals

Pius XII addressed the Cardinals on the condition of the Church after the surrender of Germany. It

Pius XII greets American sailors.

Pius XII greets American pilots.

Audience with American officers.

Pius XII welcomes doctors at an international meeting.

How exalted, how worthy of all honour is the character of your profession! The doctor has been appointed by God Himself *(cfr. Eccli. 38, 1)* to minister to the needs of suffering humanity. He who created that fever-consumed or mangled frame, now in your hands, who loves it with an eternal love, confides to you the ennobling charge of restoring it to health. You will bring to the sick-room and the operating table something of the charity of God, of the love and tenderness of Christ, the Master Physician of soul and body.

That the blessing of the King of Kings may descend upon you and your work and all your dear ones and your beloved country and remain forever, is the wish and prayer that rise from Our affectionate heart.

Extract in English of his discourse to the doctors in his own handwriting.

Pius XII meets with the Youth of Catholic Action.

was an earnest appeal for World Peace: "…Today, after six years, the fratricidal struggle has ended in one section of this war-torn world. It is a peace—if you can call it such—as yet very fragile, which cannot endure or be consolidated except by expending on it the most assiduous care; a peace whose maintenance imposes on the whole church, both pastor and faithful, grave and very delicate duties: patient prudence, courageous fidelity, the spirit of sacrifice!

"All are called upon to devote themselves to it, each in his own office and at his own place. … Would it then have been possible, by opportune and timely political action, to block once and for all the outbreak of brutal violence…? Nobody would dare to give an unqualified judgment… But in any case nobody could accuse the Church of not having denounced and exposed in time the true nature of the National Socialist movement and the danger to which it exposed Christian civilization: 'Whoever

sets up race or the people or the state or a particular form of state or the depositories' power or any other fundamental value of the human community to be the supreme norm of all, even of religious values, and divinizes them to an idolatrous level distorts and perverts an order of the world planned and created by God.'

"Continuing the work of our predecessor, we ourselves have during the war and especially in our radio messages constantly set forth the demands and perennial laws of humanity and of the Christian faith against modern scientific methods to torture or eliminate people who were often innocent.

"This was for us the most opportune—and we might even say the only efficacious—way of proclaiming before the world the immutable principles of the moral law and of confirming, in the midst of so much terror and violence, the minds and hearts of German Catholics, in the higher ideals of truth

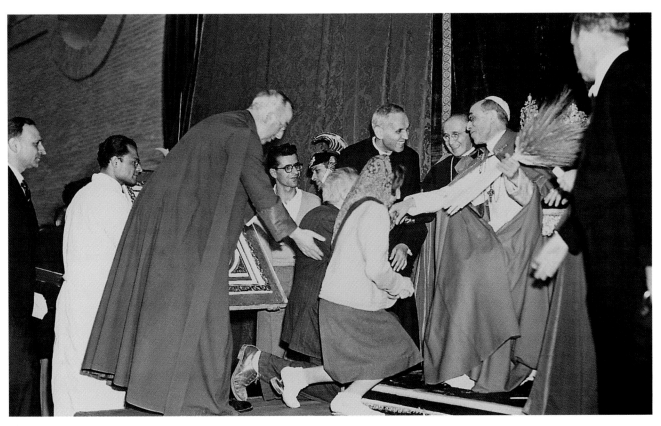

Audience with the ACLI, in the Courtyard of Belvedere.

and justice. ... The tribulations inflicted on the Church by National Socialism have been brought to an end through the sudden and tragic end of the persecution! From the prisons, concentration camps and fortresses are now pouring out, together with the political prisoners, also the crowds of those, whether clergy or laymen, whose only crime was their fidelity to Christ and to the faith of their fathers or the dauntless fulfillment of their duties as priests. But we will not lose heart. ...

"May the Holy Spirit, light of intellects, gentle ruler of hearts, deign to hear the prayers of His Church and guide in their arduous work those who in accordance with their mandate are striving sincerely despite obstacles and contradictions to reach the goal so universally, so ardently, desired: peace, a peace worthy of the name; a peace built and consolidated in sincerity and loyalty, in justice and reality; a peace of loyal and resolute force to overcome or preclude those economic and social conditions which might, as they did in the past, easily lead to new conflicts; a peace that can be approved by all right-minded men of every people and every nation; a peace which future generations may regard gratefully as the happy outcome of a sad period; a peace that may stand out in the centuries as a resolute advance in the affirmation of human dignity and of ordered liberty; a peace that may be like the *Magna Charta* which closed the dark age of violence; a peace that under the merciful guidance of God may let us so pass through temporal prosperity that we may not lose eternal happiness.[14]

"But before reaching this peace it still remains true that millions of men at their own fireside or in battle, in prison or in exile must still drink their bitter chalice. How we long to see the end of their sufferings and anguish, the realization of their hopes! For them, too, and for all mankind that suffers with

101

Rome was liberated on June 5, 1944. A huge demonstration was held as the people honored Papa Pacelli for having saved Rome from total destruction.

them and in them may our humble and ardent prayer ascend to Almighty God. Meanwhile, venerable brethren, we are immensely comforted by the thought that you share our anxieties, our prayers, our hopes; and that throughout the world Bishops, priests and faithful are joining their supplications to ours in the great chorus of the universal Church (Message of June 2, 1945)."[15]

Plaque offered by the citizens of Rome in homage to Pius XII.

January 5. 1946

L'aiuto della Chiesa Cattolica agli ebrei durante la guerra

NEW YORK, 4.

Il Direttore americano del Comitato Soccorsi in Italia, Reuben Resnik, ha dichiarato che la Chiesa cattolica si è resa altamente benemerita per il prezioso aiuto dato agli ebrei perseguitati durante la guerra. Il Resnik, secondo quanto riferisce l'INS, ha detto che tutti i membri della gerarchia cattolica in Italia, dai Cardinali ai sacerdoti, hanno salvato la vita di migliaia di ebrei, uomini, donne e bambini che furono ospitati e nascosti in conventi, chiese, istituti religiosi, case di cura per religiosi, ecc.

An article datelined New York, January 5, 1946, relates how Reubin Resnik, Director of the American Committee to Help Jews in Italy, praised the efforts of the Catholic Church for Jews during the war.

The Chief Rabbi of Rome, Israel Anton Zolli, was converted to Catholicism.

Riconoscimenti

Sul medesimo foglio americano leggiamo che durante la funzione di ringraziamento celebrata nel tempio israelitico a Roma e radiodiffusa, il cappellano israelita della quinta armata americana ha tenuto un discorso in cui tra l'altro ha detto: «Secoli fa Roma pagana festeggiava la morte apparente del popolo ebraico. Oggi in Roma cristiana la prima capitale dell'Europa non è più così.

Se non fosse stato per il soccorso veramente reale e sostanziale e l'aiuto, dato ad esso dal Vaticano e delle autorità ecclesiastiche di Roma centinaia di rifugiati e migliaia di rifugiati ebraici sarebbero indubbiamente periti molto prima che Roma fosse liberata».

An American newspaper (July 30, 1946) describes a service in a Rome synagogue after the Liberation at which a Jewish chaplain noted the "substantial assistance of the Vatican and Rome's ecclesiastical authorities" in protecting Jews.

Pius XII blesses the faithful in St. Peter's Square.

L'OSSERVATORE ROMANO

8 settembre 1945

UN MESSAGGIO DEL COMMISSARIO DELLE COMUNITA' ISRAELITICHE AGLI EBREI ITALIANI

Ieri sera giovedì, il Commissario governativo dell'Unione delle Comunità Israelitiche Italiane, dott. Giuseppe Nathan ha rivolto un appello ai suoi correligionari, iniziandosi il nuovo anno dell'era talmudica. In esso dopo aver salutata l'alba di pace nel mondo e dopo aver ricordato gl'innumerevoli israeliti trucidati e vessati dalle dittature nazi fasciste, rendendo agli scomparsi commosso omaggio, l'oratore passa ad ammonire i superstiti onde si intervorino sempre più in opere di umana solidarietà.

« Noi che abbiamo avuto la ventura di sopravvivere, abbiamo il dovere di onorare i nostri morti con un giuramento solenne, che coincida coi sacri proponimenti dei giorni di espiazione, di fare ognuno il possibile per migliorarci e migliorare tutto ciò che ci circonda, contribuire in ogni modo per rendere la nostra e la vita degli altri più apprezzabile e gradevole, per sostituire alla intolleranza ed ostilità la comprensione e la fratellanza. Dare a piene mani quanto si può per sollevare i mali e le sofferenze, assistere in tutte le maniere i bisognosi, agendo sempre con scrupolosa integrità personale e assoluta dirittura morale: in altri termini, cercare di soddisfare il proprio egoismo con opere per il bene altrui ».

Il messaggio rende poi sentite espressioni di gratitudine per quanti hanno cooperato a salvare moltissimi israeliti e ad assisterli generosamente.

Si legge, tra l'altro, nel documento: « Eleviamo la nostra commossa espressione di gratitudine a quanti nel periodo delle persecuzioni nazi-fasciste, si sono prodigati per proteggerci e per salvarci. E per primo rivolgiamo un reverente omaggio di riconoscenza al Sommo Pontefice, ai religiosi e alle religiose che, attuando le direttive del Santo Padre, non hanno veduto nei perseguitati che dei fratelli, e con slancio ed abnegazione hanno prestato la loro opera intelligente e fattiva per soccorrerci, noncuranti dei gravissimi pericoli ai quali si esponevano. Altrettanto si deve dire per le chiese ed i pastori protestanti. A tutti rinnoviamo il nostro grazie, con l'augurio che la pace si manifesti in un mondo migliore ».

Message from the Jewish Community to the Italian Jews.

105

CHAPTER VIII

Pope Pius XII and the Catholic Church

Pius XII's pontificate left a lasting mark on the history of the Catholic Church. His life was one of action, inspired by profound piety. Understanding the weaknesses of humanity, the Pope brought consolation, peace and encouragement everywhere. Striving to bring men closer to Christ, Pius XII instituted numerous liturgical reforms: the evening Mass, the new Eucharistic fast regulations and increased lay participation in liturgical functions. The Eucharistic Liturgy was the source from which Pius XII drew strength and wisdom to lead the world.

Pius XII has been called the "Pope of Mary" for his great devotion to the Mother of God, evidenced in the infallible definition of the Assumption. In his prayer to Our Lady of the Assumption, Pius XII asked her to turn her eyes "toward this world, held in the clutch of wars, persecutions, oppression of the just and the weak. And from the shadows of this vale of tears, we seek in your heavenly assistance and tender mercy comfort for our aching hearts and help in the trials of the Church, and of our fatherland. ... Comforted by our faith in future resurrection, we look to you, our life, our sweetness and our hope."

During the 1950 Holy Year, dedicated to prayer and penance, pilgrims from all over the world flocked to Rome for the opening of the Holy Door.

The Holy Father gives his blessing from the loggia of the Basilica of St. Peter.

The consecration of Russia and of the whole world to the Immaculate Heart of Mary, the solemn proclaiming of the Marian Year, the institution of the feast of the Queenship of Mary, and the proclamation of the Centenary of the Apparitions of Our Blessed Lady to St. Bernadette were also made by Pius XII.

There was a bond of friendship between the highly-cultured Pius XII, and Guglielmo Marconi who installed the Vatican Radio Station. The Pope understood all the aspects of our complex modern age. "The Church," he said, "loves and admires the progress of science in the same way that she loves art and every other thing that exalts the spirit and is for the good of man."

Pope Pius XII's conversations with the world's leaders, replete with amazing insight and comprehension, have been recorded. Of him, Dag Hammarskjöld, Secretary General of the United Nations, remarked: "In no part of the world have I ever encountered one possessing a more penetrating or complete understanding of the great problems of our time. The wisdom of his counsels will guide statesmen for years to come."

In a recently-aired interview, Los Angeles radio host Bill Handel allowed his father, a Jew, to report that he was saved by the Pope during World War II. The actions of Pope Pius XII and the Catholic Church in trying to save Jews hunted down by the

Nazis have been both praised and criticized. Pius XII was a symbol of compassion, of hope and of love during a period of lies, despair and hatred. He radiated an inner peace and beauty that inspired everyone. His goodness and spirituality deeply impressed those who knew him.

But there are others in the media who bitterly and unjustly attack Pius XII and the Catholic Church. David I. Kertzer's, *The Popes Against the Jews: the Vatican's Role in the Rise of Modern Anti-Semitism* (2001), portrays the Church as an oppressive, anti-Semitic force. Among recent books condemning Pius XII are: John Cornwell's *Hitler's Pope: The Secret History of Pius XII* (1999); Michael Phayer's *The Catholic Church and the Holocaust, 1930-1945* (1999); Gary Wills' *Papal Sin: Structures of Deceit* (1999); James Carroll's *Constantine's Sword: The Church and the Jews: A History* (2000); Susan Zuccotti's *Under His Very Windows: The Vatican and the Holocaust in Italy* (2001).

Rabbi David G. Dalin defended Pius XII and the Catholic Church in *The Weekly Standard* (February 26, 2001): "The parallel comes clear: John Paul's traditionalism is of a piece with Pius' alleged anti-Semitism; the Vatican's current stand on papal authority is in a direct line with complicity in the Nazis' extermination of the Jews. Faced with such monstrous moral equivalence and misuse of the Holocaust, how can we not object?"[16]

Dalin concludes his article calling Pius XII a "righteous Gentile." Not so, claims Kevin Madigan in his equally lenthy article, "What the Vatican Knew About the Holocaust, and When" (*Commentary*, October 2001). Madigan fails to consult the sources of Pacelli's achievements as if no testimony exists, and considers him "a very flawed human being." He does not prove his case.

Michael Novak has rightly stated: "Our faith is not in men, but in God. So there is no need for Catholics to be defensive about Pius XII. But there is need to defend the truth… . The more some of us who were earlier predisposed to blame Pius XII study this question, the better Pius XII looks and the weaker the case against him."

Speaking in St. Louis, Missouri, January 27, 1999, Pope John Paul II stated: "If you want Peace, work for Justice. If you want Justice, defend Life. If you want Life, embrace the Truth—the Truth revealed by God." Catholic apologetics must address the subject of Pope Pius XII. The evidence in his favor is incontestable.

As early as 1940, the Vatican published reports on the Church in Germany and the slaughter of Poles. Catholic defenders maintain that the Pope knew what the Nazis were doing not only to Jews, but also to Catholic priests and nuns, Gypsies, Slavs and other groups being persecuted. His strategy of helping behind the scenes was considered by his contemporaries to have been wise. He enunciated moral principles, avoided provocations, strove for impartiality among belligerents and issued information about Nazi atrocities through the Vatican Radio and the *Osservatore Romano*. In addition, he implemented the most extensive relief effort during and after the war and saved thousands of Jews and other refugees.

Pius XII spoke out many times in a strong "lonely voice." He spoke in language the whole world understood. From Santiago, Chile, the sentiments of Jews and Catholics were adequately expressed on October 3, 1943, in *El Diario ilustrado*: "…In these tragic days, our minds recall the elevated figure of the Supreme Pontiff, His Holiness Pius XII, proven defender of the cause of the persecuted, especially our millions of European brothers and sisters who are innocent victims of inhuman massacres and cruelties. We remember with indignation that those who inflict, at this present time, untold sufferings on our Holy Father, are the same forces of evil who flaunt their unspeakable attempt to imprison behind the walls of Vatican City the irrepressible winds of the immense spiritual force emanating from the Chair of Saint Peter."[17]

The Restoration of Historical Truth

Two weeks after his promise of peace, Hitler said: "One is either a German or a Christian. You cannot be both."[18] The National Socialists had a violent hatred of Jews, believed in Aryan German race superiority and called for the unification of all German-speaking peoples. Already in 1920, Clemens August Graf von Galen (the future Bishop of Münster) declared that Nazism contained ideas

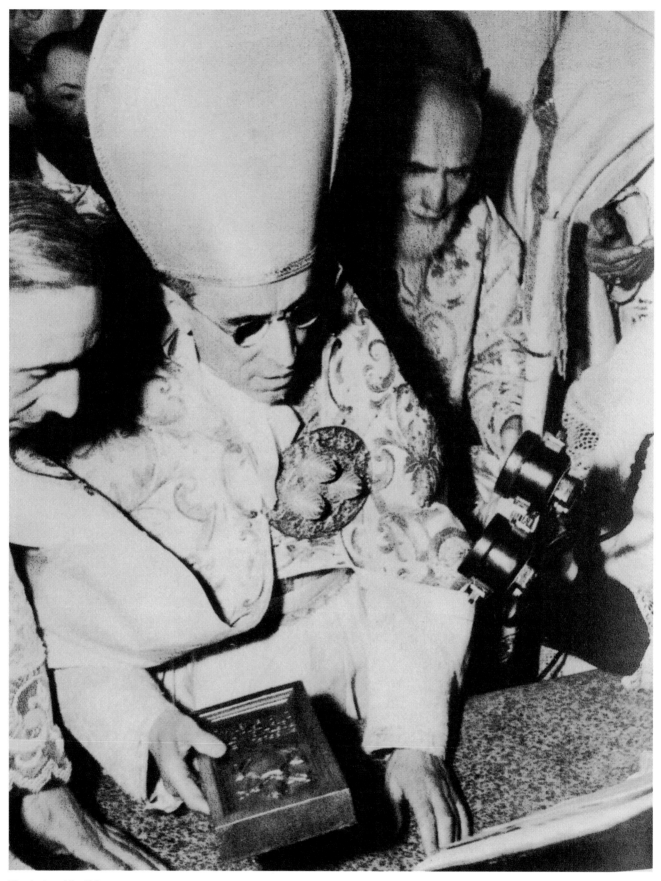

The closing of the Holy year.

Archbishop Richard J. Cushing is warmly greeted in the Vatican by Pope Pius XII during the Boston prelate's visit in 1950.

General Audience, St. Peter's, October 11, 1950, Pope Pius XII and Bishop James A. McNulty.

which no Catholic could accept without denying his faith upon cardinal points of belief.

On October 1, 1921, the *Bayerischer Kurier* quoted Nuncio Pacelli: "The Bavarian people are peace-loving. But, just as they were seduced during the revolution by alien elements—above all, Russians—into the extremes of Bolschevism, so now other non-Bavarian elements of entirely opposite persuasion have likewise thought to make Bavaria their base of operation."

Ronald J. Rychlak wrote in *Hitler, the War, and the Pope*: "This message was Pacelli's first published warning to people about Nazism, but it was not his last. Of the forty-four public speeches that Nuncio Pacelli made on German soil between 1917 and 1929, at least forty contained attacks on National Socialism or Hitler's doctrines."[19] Other Catholic leaders joined with the Nuncio. German bishops warned against Nazism on five occasions between 1920 and 1927.[20] They stated that National Socialism was totalitarian, racist, pagan, and anti-Christian."

Within a few days, the front page of *L'Osservatore Romano* (July 4, 1934) vividly described the attempted uprising, the capital executions, the various episodes of repression, and the purging of its citizens. How can critics contend that the Vatican did not speak out against Hitler's killings in Germany?

Throughout the 1930s and 1940s, the Vatican newspaper continued its condemnation of Nazism. Among the papal representatives defying the Nazis was Cardinal Pierre Gerlier, Archbishop of Lyons, who became an outspoken critic of the Vichy Government. Shortly after the Germans split France into the occupied north and unoccupied Vichy France farther south, Pius XII sent a secret letter to Catholic bishops of Europe to be read in all the Churches reminding the faithful that racism is "incompatible with the teachings of the Catholic Church."

Other courageous churchmen who defied Hitler are: two Protestants, Bishop Eivand Berggrav (Lutheran Bishop of Oslow), and Professor Karl

Audience in Castelgandolfo, October 12, 1950. Sister Francesca Cominazzi, M.P.F.,(left) presents American guests to His Holiness.

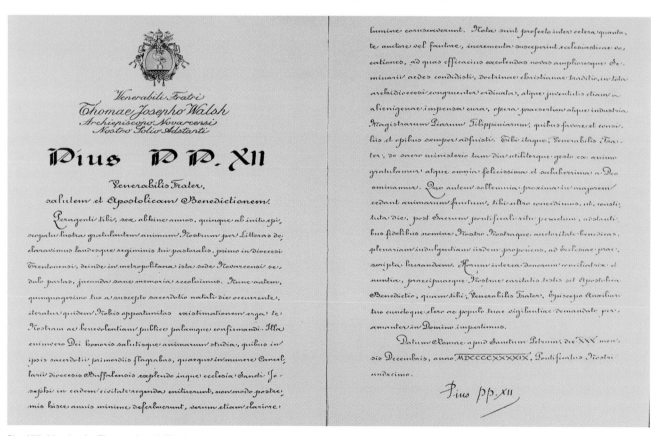

Pius XII's blessing for Thomas Joseph Walsh, the first Archbishop of Newark, New Jersey, dated December 1950.

112

Pius XII with Monsignors Richard T. Crean and John E. Grimes from the Diocese of Trenton, New Jersey.

Barth; Greek Orthodox Patriarch Gavrilo of Yugoslavia; and three Catholics: Bishop Clemens August von Galen (Bishop of Münster), Archbishop Johann de Jong (Archbishop of Utrecht), and Cardinal Ernest van Roey (Archbishop of Malines).

From the summer of 1941, the Catholic Church denounced the deportations and the treatment of Jews. On July 16, 1942, when the police rounded up 13,000 Jews in Paris, the French bishops issued a joint protest: "Our Christian conscience cries out in horror. In the name of humanity and Christian principles we demand the inalienable rights of all individuals…"

Campaign Against the Catholic Church

Increasingly, many Catholics perceive reference to Pius XII's "silence" as an insult *motivated* by anti-Catholicism. In fact, there is a tendency to refer to Pius XII's "silence," with its obvious allusion to the

In 1950, Pope Pius XII received an Italian delegation: (left) Ambassador Taliani, Minister Gonella, Honorable Andreotti, Ambassador Lupi di Soragna, Prefect Miraglia.

113

Pius XII with Arab visitors.

Shoah, and apply it to Pope John Paul II, who has done more than any other world leader to combat anti-Semitism. Dr. Eugene J. Fisher, associate director, Secretariat for Ecumenical and Interreligious Relations, National Conference of Catholic Bishops, sent a letter to the editor of the *New York Times* (May 9, 2001) stating that this troubling dimension inserted into the Jewish-Catholic dialogue needs to be confronted. The phrase, "silence of Pope Pius XII," should be "placed in the trash heap of the discarded language of racial, religious and ethnic bigotry."

The defamation and vilification campaign against Pope Pius XII continues unabated. The latest Pius XII defamer to be embraced by the media is Professor Susan Zuccotti who alleges that there are neither written records nor reliable witnesses testifying to Pius XII's efforts to save Jews. Then she proceeds either to ignore or misinterpret the massive evidence that does exist.

A telegram (No. 2341, March 9, 1944) reprinted in the book, *From Hitler's Doorstep: The Wartime Intelligence Reports of Allen Dulles, 1942-1945* contradicts Zuccotti's thesis. Jews and other refugees were hidden in the pontifical palace in Castelgandolfo when the Allies bombed the village. Nazi soldiers with heavy military equipment were stationed there

Pius XII with Japanese Ambassador and his family.

114

René Coty, President of France, visits the Holy Father.

An artist plays the violin for His Holiness.

Pius XII speaks with African Bishop.

The King of the Belgian Congo is received by Pius XII.

Patriarch Maximillian IV of the Byzantine rite greets Pius XII.

Pius XII enjoys his visitors during a General Audience.

and exchanged fire that, according to Allen Dulles, Secretary of State of the United States of America, "...resulted in the injury of about 1,000 people and the death of about 300 more. ... The Vatican protested the bombing of its territory."[21]

Susan Zuccotti simply ignores the hard evidence that is available. In her new book, *Under His Very Windows*, she does not consult 900 pages of sworn depositions for the Pope's beatification, which clearly show that he did everything possible to help Jews and other refugees during World War II. She insults Pius XII's memory and Catholic rescuers of helpless Jews, many of whom I have personally interviewed.

Another defamer is Daniel Jonah Goldhagen who wrote the controversial book, *A Moral Reckoning: the Catholic Church during the Holocaust and Today* (Knopf, 2002). The publication was preceded by *The New Republic* anti-Catholic essay of January 21, 2002. Instead of solid documentation, one finds conjectures, suppositions, insinuations. Quoted out-of-context is the April 18, 1919 letter (No. 12572) that the Apostolic Nuncio in Baveria, Archbishop Eugenio Pacelli, sent to Cardinal Gasparri in Rome. Goldhagen condemns Pacelli as an anti-Semite and claims that the letter reveals Nuncio Pacelli's antipathy toward the Jews. But it merely highlights the 1919 uprising. It is anti-revolutionary and reports a fact that the leaders of these terrorists were Bolshevik Jews from Russia, sent to Germany to foment revolution. This is a historical fact and has absolutely nothing to do with anti-Semitism. It was necessary to mention the terrorist leaders in Munich, so Pius XI would learn that the Russian Communists were seeking to extend their power in various Western countries.

I have sworn testimony from rescuers like Sister Domenica Mitaritonna who wrote: "With joy we received the Jews as our guests. ... They were welcomed by the Superior who had been solicited by the Vatican to help them."[22] Many rescuers interviewed in *Yours Is a Precious Witness: Memoirs of Jews and Catholics in Wartime Italy* (1997) agreed that they were able to respond collectively to the plight of the Jews only because the Pope had ordered them to do so.

Dr. Daniel M. Lipshutz, a young United States Army officer during World War II, was assigned to help the Pope and the Vatican in hiding and saving thousands of Jews. Alan Schneider of Fort Lee, NJ, stated that Dr. Lipshutz frequently spoke about "the Pope's courageous work as one of the great accomplishments and stories of World War II."

Is there no limit to anti-Pius criticism? Dr. Eugene Fisher wrote: "Zuccotti simply ignores the hard evidence that is available. ... Several years ago, while staying at the Sisters of Sion house in Rome, an elderly nun befriended by my then four-year-old

The Pope blesses the First Communicants.

daughter asked to see me. She wanted me to know that the Jews hidden in the convent were fed by a truck that came from the Vatican bringing food on a regular basis. The nuns could not have fed 200+ Jews for so long, of course, because of rationing. Indeed, together with the food delivery, there was always a card which read, *With the Pope's blessing for all.*"[23]

Four Hundred Visas to Jews

Just months ago (March 19, 2001), I received a letter from a man who had direct, personal knowledge of Pius XII working to save Jews by obtaining visas for them so they could escape to Latin American countries.

118

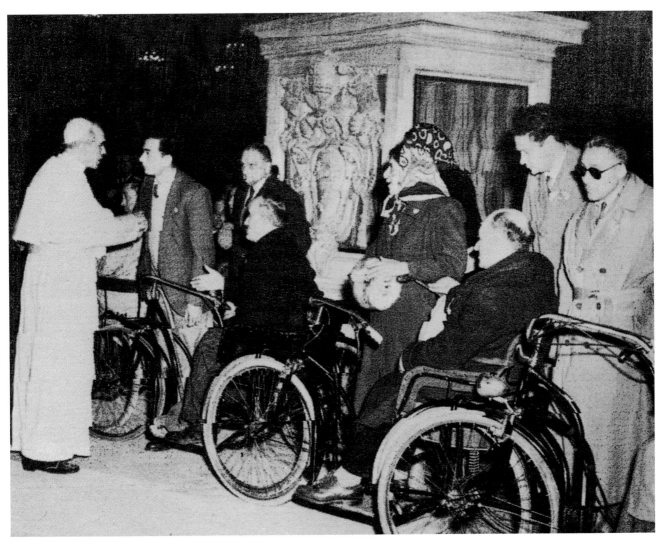

Audience with the handicapped.

As a young priest, Monsignor Giovanni Ferrofino, now retired and living in Maussane-les-Alpilles, France, was secretary to Archbishop Maurilio Silvani, Papal Nuncio to Haiti and to the Dominican Republic. Ferrofino gives us a marvelous glimpse into the way Pius XII worked to help the persecuted.

Archbishop Silvani worked closely with Eugenio Pacelli in the 1920s and 1930s in Germany. "During the war," Ferrofino writes: "I was at Port-au-Prince with Silvani who had collaborated with Vatican Secretary of State Eugenio Pacelli in Baveria during negotiations on the Concordat with Germany. In 1943, instructions came to Nuncio Silvani from Pius XII telling him to ask General Rafael Leonida Trujillo, dictator of the Dominican Republic, to grant four hundred visas to Jews. It was subsequently learned that these refugees had been refused admittance to the United States.

Nuncio Silvani immediately visited Trujillo who stated that he could not refuse the Pope. But he had conditions which Ferrofino describes. "He told us: 'None of the four hundred can remain in the capital. They must live on the frontier and protect us from

119

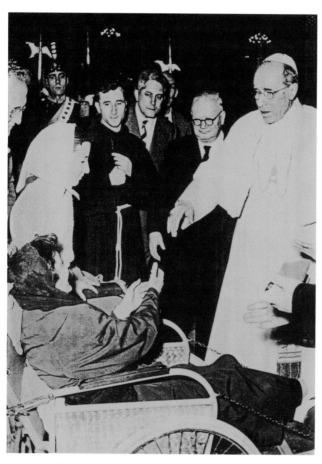
Audience with war victims.

the clandestine immigration of Haitians. They will have land, houses, everything that is needed for a well-organized colony.' A few weeks later, the four hundred Jews arrived in Santo Domingo.

"When they obtained passports from Mexico, they left clandestinely for Cuba and from that country, after a short stay there, they crossed the Mexican border and arrived safely in the United States, the land that had originally denied their entrance. All this happened, thanks to Pius XII."

It is also interesting to note that on September 19, 1942, Monsignor Paolo Bertoli, chargé d'affaires at Port-au-Prince, wrote to Cardinal Luigi Maglione, Vatican Secretary of State, informing him that General Trujillo was ready to offer hospitality to 3,500 Jewish children in France between the ages of three to fourteen. General Trujillo would organize

the group and take care of expenses for their voyage. Again, thanks to Pius XII's intercession.

Was Pius XII 'Silent?"

The charge of Pius XII's "silence" with regard to the Nazis is simply not true. In his *Diary* regarding an audience with Pope Pius XII on October 10, 1941, Angelo Giuseppe Roncalli, Apostolic Nuncio in Istanbul, declared that the Pope's statements were prudent.

In his Christmas radio messages of '41, '42, and '43 following this audience, the Pope denounced theories that attribute rights to "a particular race." He revealed that "hundreds of thousands of people, through no fault of theirs, sometimes only because of nationality or race, were destined to die."

In the book, *Pio XII: Il Papa degli Ebrei*, historian Andrea Tornielli cites the Evangelical Bishop of Berlin, Otto Dibelius: "What this Pope did or did not do, what he suffered or did not suffer, and the conflicts he conscientiously overcame before God, can be judged only by one who has had such a responsibility, and has learned what it means to profess the Christian faith and the Ten Commandments while in the frightening atmosphere of a totalitarian state and controlled by such a government."[24]

Certain Polish bishops, exiled in London, called for stronger statements by the Pontiff, while those who remained in Poland and had to deal with the Nazis, cautioned the Pope to refrain from "speaking out" against Hitler, lest his words be used as a pretext for savage reprisals. In a letter to Pope Pius XII, dated October 28, 1942, Archbishop Adam Stefan Sapieha stated: "It displeases us greatly that we cannot communicate Your Holiness' letters to our faithful, but it would furnish a pretext for further persecution and we have already had victims suspected of communicating with the Holy See."

Writing to Bishop Konrad von Preysing of Berlin, Pius XII explained: "We leave it to the local bishops to weigh the circumstances in deciding whether or not to exercise restraint, *ad maiora mala vitanda* [to avoid greater evil]. This would be advisable if the danger of retaliatory and coercive measures would be imminent in cases of public statements by the

Audience with Brides.

bishop. Here lies one of the reasons We Ourselves restrict Our public statements. The experience we had in 1942 with documents which We released for distribution to the faithful gives justification, as far as We can see, for Our attitude."

Despite Pius XII's peace efforts, the Allies would accept nothing short of Germany's unconditional surrender, even though it meant prolonging the Holocaust. John Toland reported: "The Church, under the Pope's guidance, had already saved the lives of more Jews than all other churches, religious institutions and rescue organizations combined, and was presently hiding thousands of Jews in monasteries, convents and Vatican City itself. The record of

the Allies was far more shameful. The British and Americans, despite lofty pronouncements, had not only avoided taking any meaningful action but gave sanctuary to few persecuted Jews. The Moscow Declaration of that year—signed by Roosevelt, Churchill and Stalin—methodically listed Hitler's victims as Polish, Italian, French, Dutch, Belgian, Norwegian, Soviet and Cretan. The curious omission of Jews (a policy emulated by the U.S. Office of War Information) was protested vehemently but uselessly by the World Jewish Congress. By the simple expedient of converting the Jews of Poland into Poles, and so on, the Final Solution was lost in the Big Three's general classification of Nazi terrorism." [25]

CONCLUSION

In his book, *I dilemmi e i silenzi di Pio XII*, historian Giovanni Miccoli reconstructs the facts and presents the mental attitudes, maneuvers and difficulties of the Vatican Curia during World War II. Miccoli states that the Vatican avoided taking a position that would violate its neutrality. By condemning Nazism, Pius XII would have endangered millions of Catholics and thousands of German priests. He would have jeopardized, as well, the safety of the Jews in Rome, which was the center of Fascist Italy occupied by the Germans. To take a position could have signified that the war would be transformed into a crusade... It meant going to battle with serious and dangerous consequences. Ultimately the results would block the action of persuasion, assistance and peacemaking that was the role of the pontiff.[26]

Pius XII was far from silent. In *Summi Pontificatus* (1939) and *Mystici Corporis* (1943), as well as in his Christmas messages and his June 2, 1943 address to the Cardinals, he clearly repudiated Nazi racist ideology. He ordered papal representatives to intervene in Belgium, Bulgaria, France, Greece, Holland, Hungary, Rumania, Slovakia, Spain and Turkey to stem the deportation of innocent victims to death camps. He took great risks to protect and save as many Jews as he could by sheltering them in Vatican buildings and releasing monasteries and convents from the rule of cloister.

There is no proof that a formal denunciation of Hitler and the Nazis would have been of any help to the Jews. The Church would have been treated as an enemy power and the Nazis would have invaded the Vatican and searched Catholic buildings everywhere for Jewish refugees. Pius XII's own assessment was: "No doubt a protest would have gained the praise and respect of the civilized world, but it would have submitted the poor Jews to an even worse persecution."[27]

Owen Chadwick, a well-respected British historian, wrote in *The Tablet* of London (March 28, 1998) that the propaganda against Pius XII was promoted by the Communists, "propaganda in the first instance by Stalin's men in the Cold War. ...Stalin had a political need to make this Pope contemptible."

The fact remains that Pius XII's voice was heard.

He was the object of unanimous admiration and sincere gratitude. Who can deny that Vatican Radio explicitly condemned "the immoral principles of Nazism,"[28] and the "the wickedness of Hitler" citing Hitler by name.[29] The London *Times* praised Pius XII: "There is no room for doubt. He condemns the worship of force ... and the persecution of the Jewish race."[30] *The Tablet* of London reported that Nazi leader Goebbels issued pamphlets in many languages condemning Pius XII as a "pro-Jewish Pope."[31] Jewish scholar Jenö Levai, who served as an expert witness at Adolf Eichmann's War Crimes Trial, insisted that bishops of the Catholic Church intervened again and again on the instructions of the Pope, "...the one person who did more than anyone else to halt the dreadful crime and alleviate its consequences, is today made the scapegoat for the failures of others."[32] In Monsignor Montini's *Notes*,[33] dated January 19, 1940, the Pope's intervention is clearly stated: "Pius XII ordered that information on the condition of the Church in Poland be circulated via German transmissions of Vatican Radio."

Monsignor John Patrick Carroll-Abbing, founder of Boys' Town and Girls' Town of Italy was among the Vatican officials who, at the explicit instructions of the Pope, helped shelter and feed thousands of Jews during the German occupation of Rome. He recorded the Vatican's vast rescue network in his autobiography, *But for the Grace of God*.[34]

In a taped interview with William Doino, Jr., Monsignor Carroll-Abbing recently confirmed these facts and described how the Pontiff personally ordered him and other Vatican officials to rescue Jews, and make sure to do "whatever was necessary" to allow them to practice their Jewish faith in private, according to their sacred rites. Responding to questions about the lack of papal protests, he added: "Pius XII was not silent at all! This is one of the great falsehoods of the twentieth century. He was outspoken in his condemnation of Fascist and Nazi atrocities... I worked with Fathers Pfeiffer and Benoît, as well as my assistant, Monsignor Vitucci, and Cardinals Dezza, Palazzini, Maglione, Montini and Tardini. ...I repeat, we acted on direct orders and instructions of the Holy Father."

In *Pius XII and the Second World War*, Pierre Blet concluded: "Several years later Pius XII returned to these years of fire and sword in a speech to nurses given in May 1952. He asked the question: 'What should we have done that we have not done?' The Pope was saying that he was conscious of what he had accomplished to prevent the war, to alleviate its sufferings, to reduce the number of its victims—everything he thought he could do. The documents [the *Actes*], in so far as they allow one to probe the human heart, come to the same conclusion. As for results, to affirm that the Pope himself or some other person in his place might have been able to do more is to depart from the field of history in order to venture into the undergrowth of suppositions and dreams."[35]

The vilification of the person of Pope Pius XII and the denigration of our present Pope John Paul II affects the Magisterium of the Catholic Church. Today, Catholics should promote the truth about the Holocaust—an important contemporary issue. Both Popes are accused of "silence." The Vatican chastised the Anti-Defamation League for its ads in the *New York Times* and the *International Herald Tribune*. On May 18, 2001, in a letter to Abraham Foxman obtained by *The Jewish Week*, Walter Cardinal Kasper, head of the Commission for Religious Relations with the Jews, defended John Paul II: "To defame the Holy Father by attributing 'silence' to him is quite unjust and cannot go uncontested. ...It wounds our relationship." In August, historian Peter Gumpel, representing the Vatican, denounced the "slanderous campaign" against the Catholic Church and accused some Jewish historians of "clearly incorrect behavior."

Discussion about the Pope's silence continues despite evidence that Pius XII did protest the persecution of Jews, Catholics and other victims of World War II. Paolo Mieli, a Jewish journalist, courageously defends the Catholic Church in the *Corriere della Sera*, April 26, 2002. Writing about the film *Amen* produced by Constantin Costa-Gravas, he states that "it is absurd to describe Pius XII as an accomplice of Hitler or as having any responsability for the Holocaust..."

How can anyone continue to deny the countless "testimonies" by victims of the Nazis in favor of this Pope? In the French magazine, *Reforme*, dated May 14, 2002, a protestant minister, François de Beaulieu, confirms the fact that the Nazis considered him to be "the mouthpiece of the Jewish war criminals." This new evidence contradicts the statements by Rolf Hochhuth in *The Deputy* and Costantin Costa-Gavras in the film *Amen*.

Germans were not permitted to listen to the Vatican Radio or to speak in favor of the Pope. Despite his surname, he is a German and was a young soldier working as a sergeant radio operator at the headquarters of the Wehrmacht in Zossen (near Berlin). He clandestinely transmitted Pius XII's 1942 Christmas message and circulated copies of it among his friends. In it the Pope explicitly condemned the Nazis, revealing that "hundreds of thousand of people, through no fault of theirs, sometimes only because of nationality or race, were destined to die."

Beaulieu appeared before a military tribunal on April 16, 1943. Thanks to the testimonies of his immediate superiors, he was spared the death penalty, but he was sentenced to prison for spreading a "subversive and demoralizing document." He was also accused of having a critical view of the war and of being "spiritually attracted to Jewish environments and sympathetic toward Jews."

In this article Pastor Beaulieu insists that Pius XII was not silent and that his Christmas message was understood by the Nazis. No one who has examined the record fairly can doubt that the Pope "spoke out" against the Nazi Holocaust.

On Monday, October 6, 1958, Pius XII suddenly collapsed while working at his desk. Two days later he had a second stroke. On Thursday, October 9, 1958, the Pope suffered a heart attack and died.

When Pius XII died, prayers re-echoed throughout the world. Tears were shed by millions of faithful. People in every walk of life had been inspired by him. Men, women and children of every persuasion had visited him in the Vatican. His enthusiastic bright eyes, combined with brisk step and swift movements were contagious. His personal magnetism was a blend of casualness and dignity, warmth and affection, compassion and humor. His food was frugal and limited as he dined alone while reading the newspapers at breakfast and reviewing official papers submitted by his secretaries during other meals. Though born an aristocrat, he was an ascetic.

Tributes of love and gratitude poured into Rome. The Jewish Community world-wide expressed its sorrow. "The world," President Eisenhower declared, "is now poorer following the death of the Pope." Shortly after Pius XII's death, an article in *The Jewish Newsletter* (October 20, 1958) expressed the uniqueness of his extraordinary contribution: "It is to the credit of Pope Pius XII that ... instead of preaching Christianity, as the Christian Churches had done for centuries, he and the churches practiced its principles and set an example by their acts and lives, as did the Founder of Christianity." Richard Cardinal Cushing of Boston expressed the esteem of the whole world: "Pius XII was a pastor, a good shepherd of souls, selflessly dedicated to the Church and to the greater glory of God."

Forty years after Cardinal Eugenio Pacelli became Pope, on March 18, 1979, John Paul II recalled: "I shall never forget the profound impression which I felt when I saw him close-up for the first time. It was during an audience which he granted to the young priests and seminarians of the Belgian College. Pius came to each one and when he reached me the College Rector (Monsignor Fürstenberg) told him that I came from Poland. The Pope stopped for a while and repeated with evident emotion 'from Poland'; then he said in Polish 'Praised be Jesus Christ.' This was in the first months of the year 1947, less than two years after the end of the Second World War, which had been a terrible trial for Europe, especially for Poland. On the fortieth anniversary of the beginning of this important pontificate we cannot forget the contribution that Pius XII made to the theological preparation for the Second Vatican Council, especially by his teachings on the Church, by the first liturgical reforms, by the new impetus he gave to biblical studies and by his great attention to the problems of the contemporary world."[36]

At the start of his 1987 visit to the United States, John Paul II defended Pius XII during a meeting with Jewish leaders, recalling "how deeply he felt about the tragedy of the Jewish people, and how hard and effectively he worked to assist them during the Second World War."

Pope John Paul II extended an invitation for all, Jews and Gentiles, to be united spiritually: "I hope that at the dawn of the third millennium sincere dialogue between Christians and Jews will help create a new civilization founded on the one, holy and merciful God, and fostering a humanity reconciled in love."

NOTES

[1] Shirer, *The Rise and Fall of the Third Reich*, 1959, p. 616.

[2] Cf. Charles Pichon, *The Vatican and Its Role in World Affairs.* New York, E. P. Dutton and Company, p. 167.

[3] *Ibid.*, p. 147.

[4] Cf. *Controversial Concordats*, edited by Frank Coppa. Washington, DC, the Catholic University of America Press, p. 173. Pogroms were going on in Poland. The American Jewish Committee appealed (December 30, 1915) to Pope Benedict XV to use his moral influence and speak out against anti-Semitism. Eugenio Pacelli was deeply involved in the preparation of a pro-Jewish document signed by Vatican Secretary of State Cardinal Gasparri (February 9, 1916). This statement appeared in the *New York Times*, April 17, 1916 under the headline: "Papal Bull Urges Equality for Jews." It was printed in *Civiltà Cattolica*, April 28, 1916, v. 2, pp. 358-359, and in *The Tablet*, April 29, 1916 v. 127, p. 565. Twenty years later, during his 1936 visit to America, Cardinal Pacelli met with two officials of the American Jewish Committee, Lewis Strauss and Joseph Proskauer, and re-affirmed Benedict XV's condemnation of anti-Semitism, promising to make its teaching better known. These facts are found in the archives of the American Jewish Committee, and are documented by Naomi Cohen, in her official history of the AJC, *Not Free to Desist: A History of the American Jewish Committee, 1906-1966*, The Jewish Publication Society of America (Philadelphia, 1972, pp. 180, 214-215, 578, section vii).

[5] The *New York Times*, p. 6, col. 4.

[6] The *New York Times*, January 17, 1939, p. 1, col. 3.

[7] Cf. *Actes* 8, No. 329, nota 1, p. 481, e A. Rozumek, *Die Caritas des Vatikans.*

[8] May 26, 1955.

[9] *First Things*, p. 22.

[10] *L'Osservatore Romano*, January 5, 1946.

[11] July 30, 1944. Pius XII was sympathetic to Zionism and the creation of a Jewish state, both before and after he was Pontiff, as a number of works have shown: *Three Popes and the Jews* by Pinchas Lapide (1967); *The Papacy and the Middle East* (1986); and *Christian Attitudes Toward the State of Israel* by Paul Charles Merkley (2002). (The last fifty years of conflict in the region seem to confirm Pius XII's fears of ethnic resentments and hatreds.) In 1944, Pius XII told the newly-appointed high commissioner for Palestine "of his intention not to interfere with the Jewish aspiration to create a national State in Palestine, saying that he was animated with great sympathy for the Jews." (*The Tablet* of London, Oct. 25, 1958.) And in 1945, during a meeting with Jewish survivors of the Holocaust, Pius XII told his Jewish audience approvingly: "Soon, you will have a Jewish state" (*The Jerusalem Post*, October 10, 1958).

[12] Libreria Editrice Vaticana, 1993, 2nd edition. Compelling documents vindicate Pope Pius XII. The evidence in *Actes et Documents* points to Pius XII's ceaseless activities for Peace. He was against Racism, Nationalism, Anti-Semitism and War. His efforts were on behalf of the persecuted: Jews, the homeless, widows, orphans, prisoners of war. It is important to note: 1. The Holy See's February 9, 1916 condemnation of anti-Semitism, which Eugenio Pacelli (the future Pius XII), then working in the Secretary of State's office, helped formulate. 2. The January 22, 1943 report written by the Nazi's Reich Central Security Office, which condemned Pius XII's 1942 Christmas Address for "clearly speaking on behalf of the Jews" and which accused the Pontiff of being a "mouthpiece of the Jewish War Criminals." 3. The recently discovered Nazi plan, reported in the July 5, 1998 issue of the Milan newspaper *Il Giornale*, which described Hilter's plan to "massacre Pius XII with the entire Vatican," because of the "Papal protest in favor of the Jews." The most recent followers of the anti-Pius XII myth, Susan Zuccotti (*Under His Very Windows*), Michael Phayer (*The Catholic Church and the Holocaust*) and David Kertzer (*The Popes Against the Jews*) make no mention of any of these documents in their deeply-flawed books.

[13] A.E.S. Germania 774.

[14] Cf. *Collect*, Third Sunday after Pentecost.

[15] Cf. *Acta Apostolicae Sedis*, Vol. XXIX, 1937, pp. 149 and 171. In 2003, the Vatican Archives will release files after they are properly organized and catalogued. (For two excellent essays on the Vatican's archives, which refute and respond to many anti-Catholic accusations, see Pierre Blet's 1998 article, "The Myth in Light of the Archives," reprinted in my *Pius XII: Architect of Peace*, pp. 178-189; and John Jay Hughes's article, "The Vatican Archives: What's the Problem?", *Inside the Vatican* magazine, pp. 46-49.) The material to be released will confirm that the wartime Popes, Pius XI and Pius XII were opponents of totalitarianism, and champions of peace, freedom, human dignity and love.

[16] *The Weekly Standard,* February 26, 2001. The myth of *Hitler's Pope* continues in spite of massive evidence to the contrary. Anti-Catholicism (among non-Catholics) and anti-Papalism (among disgruntled Catholics) exert a great power. The Nazi Holocaust symbolizes the most radical evil in the history of mankind, and anti-Catholics and anti-Papalists know that if they can link a Pope —in this case, Pius XII— to the Holocaust, they can forever discredit the Papacy, and the moral influence of the Church in the modern world.

[17] Rapp. nr. 3980/143 (A.E.S. 7145/43, orig.). See *Actes,* Vol. 9, p. 498.

[18] J. Derek Holmes, *The Papacy in the Modern World 1914-1978,* Crossroad, New York, 1981, p. 101.

[19] *Our Sunday Visitor,* 2000, pp. 18-19; See also, Pinchas E. Lapide, *Three Popes and the Jews: Pope Pius XII Did Not Remain Silent,* Hawthorn Books, New York, 1967, p. 118.

[20] *Op. cit.,* Holmes, p. 101.

[21] From Hitler's Doorstep: *The Wartime Intelligence Reports of Allen Dulles 1942-1945,* Pennsylvania State University Press, 1996, p. 237. See also, William Doino, "Another Distorted History of Pius XII," *Inside the Vatican,* February 2001, pp. 54-59.

[22] September 26, 2000.

[23] Letter to Margherita Marchione, May 7, 2001.

[24] Piemme, 2001, p. 199.

[25] Doubleday, New York, 1976, pp. 760-61.

[26] Rizzoli, 2000, p. 407.

[27] Quoted by Joseph L. Lichten in his Introduction to Graham, *Pius XII's Defense of Jews and Others,* pp. 2-3; See also Lapide, *Three Popes and the Jews,* p. 247.

[28] October 15, 1940.

[29] March 30, 1941.

[30] October 1, 1942.

[31] October 24, 1942.

[32] *Hungarian Jewry and the Papacy: Pius XII Was Not Silent,* Sands and Company, London, 1968.

[33] *Actes,* Vol. 3, Letter 102,

[34] Delacorte Press, 1965.

[35] Paulist Press, 1997.

[36] When Pius XII died on October 9, 1958, Padre Pio was consoled "by a vision of the former pontiff in his heavenly home," according to Padre Agostino (*Diario,* p. 225). On May 26, 2002, Elena Rossignani Pacelli confirmed this statement. With her mother, the Pope's sister Elisabetta, she visited Padre Pio who spoke about this vision. Referring to Pius XII's sanctity in his letter to Margherita Marchione (February 22, 2001), Bernard Tiffany quoted the following letter from Padre Pio's secretary, Reverend Dominic Meyer, OFM, Cap.: "Padre Pio told me he saw the Pope in Heaven during his Mass. And many miracles have been attrributed to His intercession in various parts of the world (June 30, 1959)." One of the most charismatic figures of the twentieth-century, Padre Pio, a mystic from Pietrelcina, in the province of Benevento, Italy, was beatified on May 2, 1999 and canonized on June 16, 2002.

[37] General audience of April 28, 1999. No Pope throughout history did more than Pope John Paul II to create closer relations with the Jewish community, to oppose anti-Semitism, and to make certain that the evils of the Holocaust never occur again. Relations between the Catholic Church and Jewish people are marked by mutual respect and understanding. Pope John Paul II visited the Chief Rabbi at the Synagogue in Rome in 1986 and declared that "the Jews are our dearly beloved brothers," and indeed "our elder brothers in faith." He requested forgiveness for past sins by Christians against Jews. He established full diplomatic relations between the Holy See and the State of Israel. A survivor of both Nazi and Communist oppression himself, John Paul II has consistently praised Pope Pius XII for his heroic leadership during World War II, and led the cause for his canonization.

Ten Commandments for Peace

1. Peace is always in God; God is Peace.

2. Only men who bow their heads before God are capable of giving the world a true, just and lasting peace.

3. Unite, all honest people, to bring closer the victory of human brotherhood and with it the recovery of the world.

4. Banish lies and rancor and in their stead let truth and charity reign supreme.

5. Affirm human dignity and the orderliness of liberty in living.

6. Give generously of aid and relief—State to State, people to people, above and beyond all national boundaries.

7. Assure the right of life and independence to all nations, large and small, powerful and weak.

8. Work together toward a profound reintegration of that supreme justice which reposes in the dominion of God and is preserved from every human caprice.

9. The Church established by God as the rock of human brotherhood and peace can never come to terms with the idol-worshippers of brutal violence.

10. Be prepared to make sacrifices to achieve peace.

Pius pp. XII

APPENDIX

I. Chronology of Pope Pius XII's Life

1876-1958

1876   Born in Rome of Virginia Graziosi, wife of Filippo Pacelli, March 2.

        Baptized Eugenio Maria Giuseppe Giovanni, March 4.

1880   Eugenio Pacelli entered Kindergarten, and then attended Elementary School.

1886   Received First Holy Communion.

1891   Studied at the Ennio Quirino Visconti Lyceum.

1894   Entered the Capranica Seminary in October; enrolled also at Gregorian University.

1895   Suffered a physical setback, requiring him to live at home, while continuing his studies.

        Registered in the Sapienza School of Philosophy and Letters and at the Papal Athenaeum of St. Apollinaris for Theology. He received the Baccalaureate and Licentiate degrees *summa cum laude*.

1899   Ordained a priest, April 2.

        Assigned as curate to the Chiesa Nuova.

        Continued studies for a doctorate in Canon Law and Civil Law at the Apollinaris.

1901   Served as a research aide in the Office of the Congregation of Extraordinary Ecclesiastical Affairs.

1904   Became a Papal Chamberlain with the title of Monsignor.

1905   Became a Domestic Prelate.

1910   Represented the Holy See at the Coronation of King George V in London.

1911   Appointed Assistant Secretary of the Congregation of Extraordinary Ecclesiastical Affairs, March 7.

1912   Became pro-Secretary of the Congregation of Extraordinary Ecclesiastical Affairs, June 20.

1914   Became Secretary of the said Congregation, February 1.

1917   Appointed Nuncio to Bavaria, Germany, April 20.

        Consecrated Bishop and elevated to the rank of Archbishop, May 13.

        Presented his credentials to Ludwig III, King of Bavaria, May 28.

1920   Appointed first Apostolic Nunzio of Germany, June 22.

1924   Signed a Concordat with Bavaria, March 29, ratified by the Bavarian Parliament on January 15, 1925.

1925   Left Munich for residence in Berlin.

1929   Concluded a Concordat with Prussia, June 14, ratified August 14.

        Recalled to Rome and received a Cardinal's hat on December 16.

1930   Appointed Secretary of State, February 7.

        Became archpriest of the Vatican Basilica, March 25.

1934   Presided as Papal Legate at the International Eucharistic Congress in Buenos Aires, Argentina, October 10-14.

1935   Spoke at Lourdes, April 25-28, as Pope Pius XI's delegate to France for the closing days of the jubilee year honoring the nineteenth centenary of Redemption.

1936   Arrived in the United States of America on the *Conte di Savoia*, October 8, for an "unofficial" trip covering some eight thousand miles chiefly by plane, as he made an in-depth study of the American Church.

        Invited to a luncheon at Hyde Park after President Franklin D. Roosevelt's re-election.

1937	Traveled to France in July as Cardinal-Legate to consecrate and dedicate the new basilica in Lisieux during the Eucharistic Congress.
1938	Presided at the International Eucharistic Congress in Budapest, May 25-30.
1939	Elected Pope, on March 2, taking the name of Pius XII.
	Received the papal tiara, March 12. Issued his first encyclical, *Summi Pontificatus* (On the Unity of Human Society—an attack on totalitarianism—October 20, after the Nazis' invasion of Poland, September 1).
1943	Issued *Mystici Corporis Christi*, June 29.
	Comforted the injured, administered the Last Rites, distributed money to those in need of food and clothing when American bombers dropped hundreds of tons of explosives on Rome, July 19.
	Issued *Divino Afflante Spiritu* (Biblical Studies), September 30.
1947	Issued *Fulgens Radiatur*
	(14th centenary of St. Benedict), March 21.
	Issued *Mediator Dei* (Liturgy of the Church), November 20.
1950	Defined dogma of the Assumption of the Virgin Mary, November 1, with a Papal Bull (*Munificentissimus Deus*).
	Issued *Humani Generis*, August 12.
1953	Signed a Concordat with Spain, August 27.
1956	Reformed the Holy Week Liturgy.
1957	Issued *Fidei Donum* (Future of Africa).
1958	Death of Pope Pius XII, October 9.

II. Wartime Messages

1939-1945

Much has been said and printed about Pope Pius XII's "alleged silence" over Nazi atrocities. On the other hand little appears to reveal what he did say through the Vatican Radio and what was printed in the Vatican newspaper, L'Osservatore Romano, *as well as in newspapers world-wide. The following is a partial listing of the Holy Father's messages:*

1939

August 24	Pope Pius XII pleaded for the preservation of peace among nations.
August 31	The Holy Father sent a message appealing for peace to the French, German, and Polish Ambassadors and to the British Minister.

November 10	Pius XII spoke about true peace and harmony among peoples during an audience with the Minister of Haiti.
December 24	In his Christmas Eve allocution to the Cardinals, Pius XII referred to the invasion of Poland and related events.

1940

January 2	Renewing the papal plea for peace, Pius XII sent a message to the President of the United States.
April 15	Letter to the Cardinal Secretary of State requesting that he announce publicly special prayers for the month of May.
May 11	The Pope referred to a world "poisoned by lies and disloyalty and wounded by excesses of violence," as he condemned the invasions of Belgium, Holland, and Luxemburg.
June 2	On his onomastic day Pius XII addressed the Cardinals of the Curia about the world conflict.
July 10	Pius XII spoke against the overvaluation of blood and race.
December 21	The Holy Father appealed for prayers and action to alleviate, especially among children, the sufferings caused by the war.
December 26	The Pope mentioned the work of the Holy See and pleaded for relief "to those poor people who are overcome by the sorrows and tribulations of war's calamities."

1941

March 30	Vatican Radio denounced Fascist racial theory and alluded to "the wickedness of Hitler."
April 13	In his Easter message, the Holy Father protested "atrocious forms of fighting ... and treatment of prisoners and civilians."
April 20	The Pope urged the faithful to pray for peace, especially during the month of May.
June 2	On his onomastic day, the Holy Father again manifested his concern for suffering humanity.
September 21	His Holiness announced publicly that prayers be said in honor of Our Lady of the Rosary in October.
December 24	Pius XII pleaded for the safety of "those expelled from their native land and deported to foreign lands." He stated that in the interests of the common good the rights of the smaller States should be respected—"rights to political freedom, to economic development and to the adequate use of that neutrality which is theirs according to the natural, as well as international, law. In this way, and in this way only, will they be able to obtain a fitting share of the common good, and assure the material and spiritual welfare of their people."

1942

April 15	Pope Pius XII invited all to join him in a "Crusade of prayer" to stop the massacre.
May 12	On the twenty-fifth anniversary of his episcopal consecration, he addressed the world by radio reaffirming his hope for peace.

December 24	Pius XII spoke about the "sad succession of acts at variance with the human and Christian sense." On Christmas Eve he denounced the war and emphasized reconciliation and a new internal order among the various nations. He revealed that "hundreds of thousands of people, through no fault of theirs, sometimes only because of nationality or race, were destined to die."

1943

January 25	Regarding the hardships affecting the faithful, the Pope sent a letter expressing his sorrow to the Cardinal Archbishop of Palermo, as he had already done for those of Genoa, Turin, Milan, and Naples.
June 2	Vatican Radio stated: "He who makes a distinction between Jews and other men is unfaithful to God and is in conflict with God's commands." The Pope referred to "those who, because of their nationality or their descent, are pursued by mounting misfortune and increasing suffering. ... Those who guide the fate of nations should not forget that, in the words of the Scriptures, he who bears the sword is not therefore the master over the life and death of men, unless it be according to the divine law, from whence all power derives." He also mentioned his unsuccessful negotiations on behalf of the persecuted victims.
June 21	Vatican Radio broadcast in German a long text on the rights of Jews under natural law and, a few days later, a defense of Yugoslav Jews: "Every man bears the stamp of God."
July 20	Pius XII wrote a letter to the Cardinal Vicar of Rome expressing his sorrow over the devastation of the Basilica of San Lorenzo during the bombing of Rome.
August 5	The Pope wrote to Cardinal Maglione, Vatican Secretary of State, complaining that no heed was paid to his words and his efforts to replace hatred with charity.
September 1	Four years after the beginning of the war, Pius XII's broadcast was entitled "Blessed Are the Peacemakers," in which he invoked blessings for those ready to make peace, together with a warning against giving "new life to the fire of hatred."
December 24	In his 1943 Christmas message, Pius XII stated: "We see, indeed, only a conflict which is degenerating into that form of warfare which excludes all restriction and restraint. ... It is a form of warfare which proceeds without intermission on its terrible way, and piles up slaughter of such a kind that the most bloodstained pages of history pale in comparison with it. ... Every human sentiment is crushed and the light of reason eclipsed so that the words of wisdom are fulfilled: 'They were all found together with one chain of darkness.'"

1944

March 8	In an address to the Romans, Pius XII spoke about "an air war that knows no law or restraint." He described his frustration at being unable to stop the deportations and exile of even the sick: "We recognize with bitterness of spirit how inadequate is all human help. There are misfortunes which even the most generous help of man cannot alleviate."

June 2	Two days before the Allies entered Rome, the Pope referred to "the indigence on every side and the calls for help. ...For our thoughts, day and night, are bent on our own great problem: how we may be able to meet this bitter trial, helping all without distinction of nationality or race, and how we may help towards restoring peace at last to tortured mankind."
December 24	In his Christmas broadcast to the world, Pius XII stated: " If ever a generation has had to appreciate in the depths of its heart the cry of 'War on war!', it is certainly the present generation. Having passed through an ocean of blood and tears in a form perhaps never experienced in past ages, it has lived through the inexorable atrocities with such intensity that the recollection of so many horrors must remain stamped on its memory, and even in the deepest recesses of its soul, like a picture of Hell, against which anyone who cherishes a sense of humanity desires more than anything else to close the door forever."

1945

March 19	On Passion Sunday, His Holiness spoke about the deepest cause of the terrible conflict and stated that it "is the spirit of evil which sets itself up against the spirit of God... For those who have allowed themselves to be seduced by the advocates of violence, there is but one road to salvation: to repudiate once and for all the idolatry of absolute nationalism, the pride in origin, race and blood."
May 9	In a short speech, Pius XII commented: "Kneeling in spirit before the graves and the rivers red with blood where lie the countless remains of those who fell fighting, and of the victims of massacres, hunger or misery, we commend them all in our prayers... "
June 2	In this message to the Cardinals, Pius XII is truly an Architect for Peace (cf. Part III, Pope Pius XII's Appeal for World Peace, pp. 155-163 in *Pius XII: Architect for Peace*, for the entire speech of June 2, 1945).

Su

Luisa Pretti

scenda, propiziatrice della divina pace
di Cristo, la Nostra Paterna Benedizione

Pius pp. XII

CITTÀ DEL VATICANO

CARTOLINA POSTALE
GIUBILEO DI S.S. PIO XII
Anno 1942-1943

XXV ANNIVERSARI
DELLA CONSA
EPISCOPALE DI S

CITTÀ DEL VATICANO
16-17
5 · X
1942
POSTE

POSTE VATICANE
25

Signora Luisa Pretti d'Avanzo

15 V. Fonte di Fauno

Roma

(PROV. _____)

PROPR. ART. RISERVATA - SOC. ED. VITA E PENSIERO - REPARTO R. NECCHI, 2 - MILANO
GRAFICHE A.L.M.R. BINDA, 10 MILANO

III. Selected Encyclicals and Addresses of His Holiness Pope Pius XII

Introduction to the Encyclicals

Eugenio Pacelli was Nunzio in Germany (1917-1929), then Vatican Secretary of State (1930-1939) and finally elected Pope (1939-1958).

With the publication of his writings, it became possible to understand the breadth and the importance of his words. A series of texts preceded his pontificate: A *Collection of Discourses* (Berlin, 1930) when he was Apostolic Nunzio in Germany; *Discourses and Sermons 1931-1939*, (Vatican, Tipografia Poliglotta, 1939) which were given as Secretary of State. More important from a political and religious point of view are the following: *Discourses and Radio Messages* (Vatican, Tipografia Poliglotta, 1940-1959) in 20 volumes; *Acts and Discourses* by Pius XII (Rome, Edizioni Paoline, 1940-1959), in 20 volumes.

The monumental work by Pierre Blet, Angelo Martini, Burkhart Schneider and Robert A. Graham is entitled *Actes et Documents du Saint Siège relatifs à la Seconde Guerre Mondiale*, published from 1965 to 1981 by Libreria Editrice Vaticana, I-XI (III in 2 tomes).

During the Second Vatican Council, Pius XII is quoted more than any other writer except the Sacred Scriptures. His words served the Council Fathers and show the breadth of his theology and his understanding of the needs of the Church in the 20th century. It suffices to note the variety of topics in his encyclicals.

Summi Pontificatus	October 20, 1939 *On the Function of the State in the Modern world* called for unity in opposing world evils and denounced the errors of "racism and totalitarianism."
Sertum Laetitiae	November 1, 1939 *To the Church in the United States* praised the progress of the Church in America and urged Catholics to adhere more strictly to Catholic life and principles.
Mystici Corporis Christi	June 29, 1943 *The Mystical Body of Christ* attacked National Socialism: "The Church of God is despised and hated by those who shut their eyes to the light of Christian wisdom and miserably return to the teachings, customs and practices of ancient paganism."
Divino Afflante Spiritu	September 30, 1943 *Inspired by the Divine Spirit* defined the most opportune way to promote Biblical studies.
Papal Directives for the Woman of Today	September 11, 1947 *Allocution of Pope Pius XII* addressing the Congress of the International Union of Catholic Women's Leagues, Rome, Italy: "Women must safeguard the rights of the family and participate in the social and political life of the world."

Fulgens Radiatur	March 21, 1947 *Fulgens Radiatur* expressed the need for the restoration of the Abbey of Montecassino, destroyed in World War II, and that served as a symbol of faith in an unstable world.
Mediator Dei	November 20, 1947 *On Sacred Liturgy* attempted to secure and to inculcate all that is good in the liturgical movement and to delete the unsound principles and practices.
Humani Generis	August 12, 1950 *Humani Generis* concerned some false opinions which threatened to undermine the foundations of Catholic Doctrine. It warned against minimizing the importance of dogma in an attempt to make Catholic teaching more acceptable to non-Catholics.
Menti Nostrae	September 23, 1950 *Apostolic Exhortation* to the clergy of the entire world on the development of holiness in Priestly Life.
Munificentissimus Deus	November 1, 1950 *On the Dogma of the Assumption* that Mary, the Virgin Mother of God, was assumed, body and soul, into the glory of heaven.
Evangelii Praecones	June 2, 1951 *On promoting Catholic Missions* "that the word of God may reach its aim triumphantly," on the occasion of the 25th anniversary of the Encyclical Letter *Rerum Ecclesiae*.
Moral Questions Affecting Married Life	October 29, 1951 and November 26, 1951 *Addresses* given to the Italian Catholic Union of Midwives and to the National Congress of the Family Front.
Fulgens Corona	September 8, 1953 *On the Marian Year* and on the centenary of the definition of the Dogma of the Immaculate Conception.
Sacra Virginitas	March 25, 1954 *On Holy Virginity* confirms the sublimity of the celibate state and the error of advocation of marriage as a higher state.
Ad Caeli Reginam	October 11, 1954 *On the Queenship of Mary* states that Mary reigns with her maternal heart over the entire world, just as she is crowned with the diadem of royal glory in heavenly blessedness.

Haurietis Aquas	May 15, 1956
	On Devotion to the Sacred Heart begins with the words of the Prophet Isaias: "You shall draw waters with joy out of the Savior's fountains."
Miranda Prorsus	September 8, 1957
	On the moral questions involved in Radio, TV and Motion Pictures.
Guiding Principles of the Lay Apostolate	October 5, 1957
	Pope Pius XII addressed the Second World Congress of the Lay Apostolate: "Christ's Church has no intention of yielding ground to her avowed enemy, atheistic communism, without a struggle. This battle will be fought to the end, but with the weapons of Christ!"
The States of Perfection	December 12, 1957
	On the States of Perfection was addressed to the Second General Congress, which tightened the bonds uniting organizations among themselves and with the Holy See.
Applied Psychology	April 10, 1958
	On Psychotherapy and Religion was addressed to the Fifth International Congress on Psychotherapy and Clinical Psychology.
Sacred Music and the Sacred Liturgy	September 3, 1958
	Instructions of the Sacred Congregation of Rites were approved by Pius XII.

ICONOGRAPHY

Introduction

During World War II, Pius XII's goodness and spiritual strength impressed the pilgrims who visited him. They recognized his intelligence and his extraordinary capacity to understand the sufferings and the dangers of people everywhere. He was a person who radiated an interior peace and a spiritual beauty that inspired his visitors. He was an exceptional and saintly individual, a symbol of mercy, of hope and of love, during a period in history full of lies, desperation and hatred.

It suffices to study the testimonials given by contemporaries who heard his words. He spoke of freedom, education, economic and social problems. He left us a legacy that offers valid evidence of his ecumenism. In fact, he spoke of brotherhood, of love, and of peace among religious groups. His message was a source of inspiration. He was a sacred messenger, who tried to unite and to bring peace to the whole world. His words of wisdom and indefatigable works translated, as no other person, the message of Christ, in a period of spiritual poverty and of material destruction of exceptional dimensions.

When Adolf Hitler was nominated Chancellor of Germany on January 30, 1933, the first official step taken by the Vatican Secretary of State, Cardinal Eugenio Pacelli, who six years later would become Pope Pius XII, was to defend the Jews.

An article by Robert Leiber, SJ, "Mit brennender Sorge," demonstrates clearly that the Holy See informed the Apostolic Nunzio in Berlin to "officially represent the Vatican defense of the Jews with the German Government and to alert the Nazis about the dangers of antisemitic politics."

This crucial information contradicts the thesis that Cardinal Pacelli did not defend the Jews. It is clear that throughout his life, Pius XII was endowed with great sensitivity and a spirit of brotherhood toward the Jews and proves that he was not antisemitic.

"A picture is worth a thousand words." In pursuing this research, I could think of no better means of presenting the truth to the general public than through the use of photography. Words cannot describe the tensions and sufferings Pius XII experienced during World War II. About two hundred photographs were selected from a thousand that represent different circumstances and occasions and include the important personalities who met Pius XII during his long life, before and after his pontificate. In general the media acknowledged Pius XII as a great personality, worthy to be followed and photographed on his trips throughout the world. During his lifetime, he was appreciated and venerated. In this collection he is presented as a *Shepherd of Souls*, dedicated to his duties toward the Church and to the glory of God. Posterity will evaluate and judge the past.

In a special way one should note the precious colored sketches from *La Domenica del Corriere, La Domenica degli Italiani,* and *La Tribuna Illustrata.* The photographs are from the Archives of *L'Osservatore Romano* and *Foto Felici,* others are from the *Annuario Pontificio* and from out-of-print books; United States Holocaust Memorial Museum, Washington, DC; from the Archives of the Archdiocese of Baltimore and St. Paul-Minneapolis, Diocese of Trenton, NJ, Knights of Columbus, Religious Teachers Filippini, Catholic University of America, Fordham, Notre Dame, and Seton Hall University.

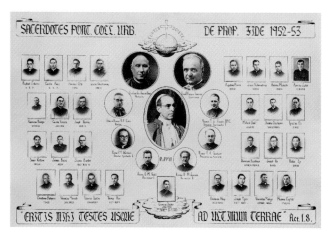

In 1953, in the presence of the American Hierarchy, the Pope dedicated the new North American College in Rome.

TO OUR BELOVED SONS, THE CARDINAL ARCHBISHOPS, AND TO OUR VENERABLE BRETHREN, THE ARCHBISHOPS, BISHOPS, AND LOCAL ORDINARIES OF THE UNITED STATES OF AMERICA HAVING COMMUNION WITH THE APOSTOLIC SEE

PIVS PP. XII

BELOVED SONS AND VENERABLE BRETHREN

THE APPROACHING REESTABLISHMENT HERE IN OUR DEAR ROME OF THE NORTH AMERICAN COLLEGE THE KNOWLEDGE OF WHOSE REOPENING HAS BEEN COMMUNICATED TO US BY THE RECTOR, AFFORDS US THE WELCOME OPPORTUNITY OF ADDRESSING OUR PATERNAL WORDS TO YOU, THE MEMBERS OF THE HIERARCHY OF THE UNITED STATES. WE REJOICE NOT ONLY IN THE FACT THAT AFTER A LAPSE OF EIGHT YEARS YOU ARE ONCE MORE SENDING YOUR CHOSEN YOUNG MEN TO STUDY IN OUR BELOVED CITY, TO IMBIBE THE SACRED WISDOM OF HOLY MOTHER THE CHURCH AT ITS VERY SOURCE, AND TO BE NOURISHED AT THE VERY HEART OF THE CATHOLIC WORLD, BUT THAT YOU ARE ALSO PLANNING TO ERECT IN THE VERY SHADOW OF OUR OWN DWELLING A NEW AND GREATER SEMINARY TO CARE FOR EVER MORE YOUNG LEVITES FROM AMERICA. IT WAS OUR PREDECESSOR OF BLESSED MEMORY, PIUS IX, WHO NEARLY ONE HUNDRED YEARS AGO FIRST PROPOSED TO THE AMERICAN BISHOPS THAT THEY ESTABLISH A NATIONAL SEMINARY IN ROME, AND IT WAS THE SAME PONTIFF WHO PURCHASED AND GRACIOUSLY GRANTED THE USE OF THE EDIFICE THAT HAS HOUSED THE AMERICAN STUDENTS EVER SINCE THAT TIME.

SURELY THERE IS EVIDENT THE HAND OF DIVINE PROVIDENCE IN THE FACT THAT THE FIRST STEPS WERE TAKEN ON THE OCCASION OF THE DEFINITION OF THE DOGMA OF THE IMMACULATE CONCEPTION AND THAT THE COLLEGE ITSELF WAS OPENED FOR THE FIRST TIME ON THE VERY EVE OF THE FEAST ON DECEMBER 7TH 1859, AND SINCE THAT DAY OUR HEAVENLY MOTHER, QUEEN OF THE CLERGY, HAS NEVER CEASED TO BLESS WITH EVERY MANIFESTATION OF DIVINE FAVOR A WORK THAT IS OF NECESSITY SO CLOSE TO HER MATERNAL HEART, THE STUDENTS NURTURED IN TENDER LOVE OF THEIR MOTHER AND QUEEN, DEVELOPED IN THE IMAGE OF HER DIVINE SON, ENLIGHTENED IN THE SACRED SCIENCES LEARNED AT THE FEET OF CHRIST'S VICAR, MADE STRONG AND COURAGEOUS BY THEIR CLOSE ASSOCIATION WITH THE PLACES SANCTIFIED BY THE PRINCE OF THE APOSTLES AND THE MARTYRS, HAVE RETURNED TO THEIR OWN COUNTRY TO WIN EVER GREATER TRIUMPHS FOR CHRIST AND HIS HOLY SPOUSE AS PASTORS AND TEACHERS, AS ADMINISTRATORS AND ALSO AS BISHOPS OF THE CHURCH IN AMERICA. THE MEN TRAINED HERE HAVE ALWAYS BEEN MARKED WITH AN ESPECIAL LOYALTY TO US AND TO OUR ILLUSTRIOUS PREDECESSORS, AN INEVITABLE CONSEQUENCE OF THEIR SOJOURN IN THIS CITY, THE SEE OF PETER AND OF PETER'S SUCCESSORS.

TODAY AS WE LOOK ABOUT THE CITY OF ROME WE SEE ON ALL SIDES THE FLOWER OF THE YOUTH OF THE WORLD, EVEN FROM THE MOST DISTANT NATIONS DRAWN HERE BY A COMMON FAITH, SUSTAINED BY COMMON IDEALS BEING TRAINED IN THE SAME DOCTRINE, SHARING THE SAME DIVINE SACRIFICE, AND ALL UNITED BY THE SAME BONDS OF ATTACHMENT TO US. SURELY THEY ARE GIVING TO THE LEADERS AND TO THE PEOPLES OF EVERY LAND A MAGNIFICENT EXAMPLE OF UNITY AND OF THE ABILITY OF MANKIND TO LIVE TOGETHER IN CHRISTIAN PEACE AND CONCORD. THE CONCURRENCE OF SO MANY THOUSANDS OF MEN, LATER DESTINED TO PLAY SUCH AN IMPORTANT PART IN THE SALVATION OF SOULS OVER THE WHOLE FACE OF THE EARTH, IS A GREAT CONSOLATION TO US AND IT SHOULD BE TO YOU, BELOVED SONS AND VENERABLE BRETHREN, A REASON ESPECIALLY APPEALING AT THIS TIME TO BE PROMPT IN MAKING EVERY SACRIFICE NECESSARY TO MAINTAIN AND EVEN TO ENLARGE THE NATIONAL SEMINARY OF YOUR COUNTRY.

SO IT IS WITH PARTICULAR JOY THAT WE HAVE LEARNED OF YOUR PROPOSALS TO ERECT AN EVEN FINER SEMINARY AND TO PLANT YOUR ROOTS EVEN CLOSER TO US. YOUR WISDOM AND COURAGE TO LOOK TO THE FUTURE AND TO PLAN FOR ALMOST THREE HUNDRED OF YOUR SEMINARIANS TO STUDY IN ROME REPRESENT A MOST WORTHY INITIATIVE THAT CAN ELICIT ONLY OUR WARMEST COMMENDATION. AT THE SAME TIME YOU ARE KEEPING A CLOSE TIE WITH YOUR OLD AND HONORED TRADITIONS IN PUTTING THE FORMER COLLEGE BUILDING TO USE AS A HOUSE OF STUDIES FOR PRIESTS WISHING TO TRAIN THEMSELVES IN THE HIGHER BRANCHES OF THE SACRED SCIENCES. BOTH OF THESE PROJECTS CALL FORTH OUR HEARTIEST APPROVAL AND SUPPORT AND THE RETURN IN GRACE AND WISDOM THAT WILL ACCRUE TO THE CHURCH IN AMERICA WILL AMPLY REWARD THE EXPENDITURES AND SACRIFICES THAT ARE NECESSARILY INVOLVED IN THEIR REALIZATION.

THE UNITED ACTION TAKEN IN THIS MATTER BY THE AMERICAN HIERARCHY, ALWAYS SO READY AND GENEROUS IN THEIR SUPPORT OF ALL MEASURES FOR THE EXTENSION OF THE KINGDOM OF CHRIST, ONCE MORE DEMONSTRATES THE FLOURISHING CONDITION OF THE FAITH IN YOUR GREAT NATION. WE ARE SURE THAT THE BISHOPS AND PRIESTS AND PEOPLE WILL RALLY TO THE SUPPORT OF A CAUSE THAT PROMISES SO MUCH FOR THE CHURCH AND WHICH IS SO CLOSE TO OUR OWN HEART. ALREADY AN ABUNDANT AND FRUITFUL HARVEST FOR GOD AND FOR SOULS HAS BEEN GARNERED FROM THE PAST EIGHTY-NINE YEARS OF THE EXISTENCE OF THE NORTH AMERICAN COLLEGE, AND NOW YOUR DECISIONS FOR THE FUTURE GIVE ABUNDANT HOPE THAT SUCCEEDING GENERATIONS WILL CONTINUE, IN GREATER MEASURE AND WITH MORE AMPLE FACILITIES, TO ENJOY THE RICHEST BLESSINGS STEMMING FROM A PRIESTHOOD NOURISHED IN THE ETERNAL CITY.

WITH GREAT JOY THEN WE GIVE OUR BLESSING TO THE PLANS THAT HAVE BEEN MADE KNOWN TO US BY THE RECTOR FOR THE FUTURE OF YOUR SEMINARY. WE SHALL FOLLOW THEIR UNFOLDING AND THEIR REALIZATION WITH INTIMATE PLEASURE AND PERSONAL INTEREST AND, AS A TOKEN OF OUR ENCOURAGEMENT IN THE GREAT TASK THAT LIES AHEAD, WE IMPART TO YOU BELOVED SONS AND VENERABLE BRETHREN, AS ALSO TO THE PRIESTS AND FAITHFUL OF THE UNITED STATES, OUR PATERNAL APOSTOLIC BENEDICTION.

GIVEN AT THE VATICAN ON THE EIGHTEENTH DAY OF FEBRUARY ONE THOUSAND NINE HUNDRED AND FORTY EIGHT, THE NINTH YEAR OF OUR PONTIFICATE.

PIVS PP. XII

PIVS·XII·PONT·MAX·HAS·AEDES·PRAESENS·DICAVIT·PRID·ID·OCT·A·MCMLIII

Inscription at the North American College in Rome

Inscription at the North American College.

May 1955: Pius XII with His Excellency Amleto Giovanni Cicognani, Apostolic Delegate (1933-1978), Monsignor Robert Hagerty, Secretary, Cardinal Pio Laghi, then secretary of the Delegation in Washington, DC.

In gratitude for having saved so many Jews, on May 26, 1955, the Israeli Philharmonic performed Beethoven's Seventh Symphony in the presence of Pius XII.

Elena Rossignani Pacelli (the Pope's niece) and Sister Margherita Marchione during the baciamano in Saint Peter's Basilica in July 1957.

Pope John Paul II examines the jacket for Italian translation of *Pius XII: Architect for Peace.*

Sister Margherita meets with John Paul II as she celebrates her Golden Jubilee.

October 1957: Pius XII blesses and inaugurates the new radio station at Santa Maria di Galeria.

Pius XII welcomes his guests.

Pius XII inspires his listeners.

Pius XII and Cardinal Angelo Roncalli, who became his successor on October 28, 1958.

Pius XII and Bishop Fulton J. Sheen.

Gary Cooper, his daughter Maria and Mrs. Cooper kissing the Pope's ring.

Pius XII and Dr. Theodor Heuss.

Pius XII and Konrad Adenauer with his daughter.

His Holiness at the Academy of Sciences.

The Pope blesses the ambulances donated by American Catholics.

Pius XII with Herbert Clark Hoover, President of the United States of America.

Pius XII with Dag Hammarskjöld, Secretary of the United Nations in Rome, April 1957.

Pius XII with Blessed Cardinal Schuster on his right.

Pius XII with Cardinal Michael Faulhaber.

Pius XII drew strength and wisdom to lead the world from the Holy Mass and the Eucharist.

The Pope was an inspiration to all as he celebrated Mass.

His Holiness prays at the tomb of St. Peter, Prince of the Apostles.

Pius XII with Monsignor Montini, the future Pope Paul VI.

Pius XII and the diplomats accreditated to the Holy See in Castelgandolfo on November 19, 1953.

1958 Medals of Pius XII.

Pius XII walked as he prepared his talks.

The last time Pius XII prayed in his chapel was on October 5, 1958.

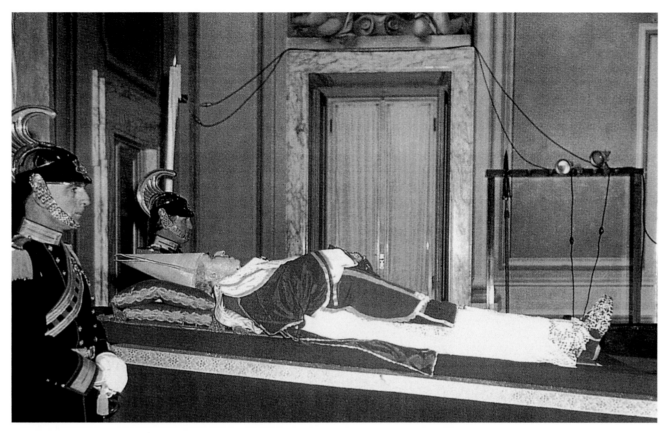

His remains were first viewed in Castelgandolfo.

At the funeral, right to left: Mother Pascalina Lehnert, the Honorable Andreotti, the Marquis Sacchetti, Mayor Cioccetti of Rome, the Pope's nephews Marcantonio and Giulio with their wives.

Monument erected in San Lorenzo Square on July 19, 1967.

Dopo l'incursione su Roma. - Il Pontefice visita le rovine della Basilica di San Lorenzo fuori le Mura, s'inginocchia a pregare e poi benedice la folla.

(Disegno di A. Beltrame)

After the devastation of the Basilica of San Lorenzo during the bombing of Rome, the Holy Father blessed the people and distributed funds to the needy.

LA DOMENICA DEGLI ITALIANI

| Anno . . . . ITALIA L. 570,- ESTERO L. 600,-
Semestre . . . . » 320,- » 340,-
Per le inserzioni rivolgersi all'Amministrazione
del Corriere d'informazione - Via Solferino, 28 -
Milano.   M | *Si pubblica a Milano ogni settimana*
Supplemento illustrato del " Corriere d'informazione "
Spedizione in abbonamento postale - Gruppo 2 | UFFICI DEL GIORNALE:
VIA SOLFERINO N. 28 - MILANO
Per tutti gli articoli e illustrazioni è riservata la
proprietà letteraria e artistica, secondo le leggi
e i trattati internazionali. |

Anno II — N. 5   3 Febbraio 1946   L. 12. — la copia

Cinquantamila fanciulli romani intorno al Papa, nella basilica di San Pietro.

Over 50,000 children surround the Pope in the Basilica of St. Peter.

LA DOMENICA DEL CORRIERE

Supplemento settimanale illustrato del nuovo CORRIERE DELLA SERA - Abbonamenti: Italia, anno L. 700, sem. L. 375 - Estero, anno L. 1000, sem. L. 525

Anno 49 — N. 30   27 Luglio 1947   L. 15 (Arretrati L. 25)

Attori dal Pontefice. Eduardo e Titina De Filippo - con la loro Compagnia - ricevuti privatamente dal Papa nella Biblioteca Vaticana: durante l'udienza, Titina De Filippo recita la "preghiera alla Vergine" della commedia "Filumena Marturano". (Disegno di W. Molino)

The actors, Edoardo and Titina De Filippo, were received privately by Pius XII in his library. Titina recited "The Prayer to the Virgin" from the comedy Filumena Marturano.

161

LA DOMENICA DEL CORRIERE

Supplemento settimanale illustrato del NUOVO CORRIERE DELLA SERA - Abbonamenti: Italia, anno L. 930, sem. L. 500, - Estero, anno L. 1230, sem. L. 650

Anno 49 — N. 34   24 Agosto 1947   L. 20 (Arretrati L. 30)

« Sinite parvulos venire ad me ». Il Papa, in villeggiatura a Castel Gandolfo, riceve e benedice, nei magnifici giardini, due bimbi accompagnati dalla madre. (Disegno di W. Molino)

Vedere articolo a pag. 5

"Sinite parvulos venire ad me" ("Let the little children come to me"). In the magnificent gardens of Castelgandolfo, Pius XII blesses a mother with her two children.

LA DOMENICA DEL CORRIERE

Supplemento settimanale illustrato del nuovo CORRIERE DELLA SERA - Abbonamenti: Italia, anno L. 1165, sem. L. 625 - Estero, anno L. 1765, sem. L. 925

Anno 50 — N. 52   26 Dicembre 1948   L. 25,—

Luigi Einaudi, Presidente della Repubblica, a colloquio col Pontefice nella Sala del Tronetto, in Vaticano.

(Disegno di W. Molino)

Luigi Einaudi, President of the Republic of Italy, meets with Pius XII in the Vatican.

164

L'ANGELICO PASTORE VEGLIA CONSOLA ILLVMINA

"Fotocolor Grafitalia"

165

La Tribuna illustrata

Anno LVIII - N. 25   Roma, 18 giugno 1950   L. 30 —

LA FESTA DEL «CORPUS DOMINI» PER L'ANNO SANTO A ROMA.
IL PAPA IN PIAZZA SAN PIETRO ALLA PROCESSIONE EUCARISTICA

A pagina 7 l'articolo: "Il Corporale sanguigno di Bolsena".

Vedere nell'interno il bando del nuovo Concorso-referendum, dotato di vistosi premi.

The Pope is depicted during the Holy Year procession on the feast of "Corpus Domini" in St. Peter's Square.

IN PIAZZA SAN PIETRO, ALLA PRESENZA DI CINQUANTA CARDINALI, DI SEICENTO VESCOVI E DI UN' INNUMEREVOLE FOLLA DI FEDELI, IL PAPA DEFINISCE IL NUOVO DOGMA DELL' ASSUNZIONE DELLA VERGINE.

(Disegno di SARO BELLOMIA)

In the presence of 50 cardinals, 600 bishops and thousands of visitors, the Holy Father proclaimed the dogma of the Assumption of the Blessed Mother.

LA DOMENICA DEL CORRIERE

Supplemento settimanale illustrato del nuovo CORRIERE DELLA SERA - Abbonamenti: Italia, anno L. 1165, sem. L. 625 - Estero, anno L. 1765, sem. L. 925

Anno 52 — N. 53   31 Dicembre 1950   L. 25,—

L'udienza più commovente dell'Anno Santo. Quattrocento pastori dell'Italia centrale hanno fatto visita al Papa, salutandolo, al suono di cornamuse e pifferi, col canto della pastorale natalizia "Tu scendi dalle stelle „. E il Pontefice si è unito al coro, modulando a bassa voce le dolci strofe. (Dis. di G. De Gaspari)

In a touching ceremony of the Holy Year, the Pope blesses a group of 400 shepherds from Central Italy who greet him with playing and singing the traditional Christmas carol, "*Tu scendi dalle stelle*". Pius XII joins them singing softly.

The Pope celebrates Holy Mass in St. Peter's Basilica.

LA DOMENICA DEL CORRIERE

Supplemento settimanale illustrato del nuovo CORRIERE DELLA SERA · Abbonamenti: Italia, anno L. 1400, sem. L. 750 · Estero, anno L. 2000, sem. L. 1050

Anno 53 — N. 43   28 Ottobre 1951   L. 30.—

Una straordinaria visione del Papa. Il cardinale Tedeschini, legato pontificio alle celebrazioni del santuario di Fatima (Portogallo), ha narrato che nell'ottobre 1950 Pio XII, mentre passeggiava da solo nei giardini vaticani, vide per tre volte, sostenendone senza pena lo splendore, il sole trasformarsi in un disco d'argento e mettersi a ruotare su se stesso, proiettando in tutte le direzioni fasci di luce con colori cangianti: lo stesso meraviglioso fenomeno manifestatosi a varie persone parecchi anni fa, appunto nel paese di Fatima. (Disegno di Walter Molino)

According to Cardinal Tedeschini, papal legate for the Fatima Celebrations, while walking in the Vatican gardens in October 1950, Pius XII witnessed the same phenomenon that took place in Fatima (the sun transformed into a silver globe rotating three times).

177

HOLY

YEAR

1950

179

Mosaic depicting Pius XII praying in the National Shrine of the Immaculate Conception in Washington, DC.

La Tribuna illustrata

••• Anno LXII - N. 50   12 dicembre 1954   Lire 30

Domenica 5 dicembre 1954: « Ai figli Nostri carissimi della diletta Roma che sentiamo così vicini nelle preghiere, come siamo Noi vicini al Maestro nelle sofferenze e nel compiere la Sua volontà, come sempre buona e benefica, impartiamo, col cuore rivolto al Signore e alla Vergine Immacolata, la Nostra paterna, apostolica benedizione ». Il Santo Padre debole, infermo, ha trovato la forza di salutare, con queste parole i fedeli.

Although not feeling well, the Holy Father addressed the people of Rome and gave the Apostolic Blessing on Sunday, December 5, 1954.

LA DOMENICA DEL CORRIERE

Supplemento settimanale illustrato del nuovo CORRIERE DELLA SERA - *Abbonamenti: Italia, anno L. 1400, semestre L. 750 - Estero, anno L. 2350, semestre L. 1250*

Anno 58 — N. 43   21 Ottobre 1956   L. 30.—

Iascia o raddoppia" a Castelgandolfo. Parecchi dei più popolari personaggi del quiz televisivo, accompagnati
i presentatori Mike Bongiorno ed Edy Campagnoli, sono stati ricevuti in udienza dal Papa, che si è tratte-
to con loro affabilmente per alcuni minuti. In questo disegno, cominciando da sinistra in basso, si riconoscono:
le Gallotti (cinema), Luciano Zeppegno (architettura), Adriano Anici (storia romana), Anna Maria Barbato
nzoni), Lando Dègoli (lirica), Attilio Zago (teatro), Giancarla Lucchini (architettura), Edy Campagnoli (presenta-
e), Remo Cappelli (numismatica), Walter Marchetti (musica moderna), Egidio Cristini (Omero), Mario De Maria
lismo) e Ugo Rossi (gastronomia). Nel centro, di fronte al Pontefice, Mike Bongiorno.   (Disegno di Walter Molino)

The Pope receives Mike Bongiorno and other TV personalities in Castelgandolfo.

LA DOMENICA DEL CORRIERE

Supplemento settimanale illustrato del nuovo *CORRIERE DELLA SERA* - Abbonamenti: *Italia, anno L. 1400, semestre L. 750 - Estero, anno L. 2350, semestre L. 1250*

Anno 59 — N. 3   20 Gennaio 1957   L. 30.—

Bimba prodigio in Vaticano. Nella Sala del Tronetto S.S. Pio XII ha ricevuto Minou Drouet, la piccola poetessa che nel settembre del 1955, quando aveva solo otto anni, strabiliò critici e lettori francesi con la pubblicazione di un volume di poesie bellissime. Molti allora dubitarono che i versi fossero suoi e li attribuirono a Claude Drouet, la signorina anziana che l'aveva adottata, dopo averla tolta da un ospizio di trovatelli a Parigi. Poi questi dubbi si dissiparono. Il Sommo Pontefice alla fine dell'udienza ha regalato alla bimba un rosario d'oro. (Disegno di Walter Molino)

In September 1955, Pope Pius XII received the eight-year-old Minou Drouet, French child prodigy whose poetry was acclaimed by the critics, and gave her gold rosary beads.

LA DOMENICA DEL CORRIERE

Supplemento settimanale illustrato del nuovo *CORRIERE DELLA SERA* - Abbonamenti: Italia, anno L. 1870, semestre L. 1000 - Estero, anno L. 2805, semestre L. 1470

Anno 59 — N. 19   12 Maggio 1957   L. 40.—

Ranieri e Grace dal Papa. Durante il loro viaggio in Italia, il principe di Monaco e sua moglie sono stati ricevuti in forma solenne, nella Sala del Tronetto in Vaticano, dal Pontefice che si è intrattenuto con essi per una ventina di minuti. All'uscita, in piazza San Pietro, una folla ha accolto calorosamente i due principi per i quali il pubblico romano ha eccezionalmente dimenticato la tradizionale indifferenza.

(*Disegno di Walter Molino*)

Prince Ranieri and Princess Grace of Monaco receive a very warm welcome. Their visit with the Pope lasted more than twenty minutes.

Affresco by Ferruccio Ferrazzi.

Smiling, the Holy Father greets his people from the Sedia Gestatoria.

MEDALS COINED BY THE ITALIAN MINT
IN HONOR OF POPE PIVS XII

D/ PIVS - XII - PONTIFEX - MAXIMVS - A - I
Bust of the Pontiff facing left with zucchetto, mozzetta and stole; under the bust: MISTRUZZI

1939 - ELECTION TO THE PAPACY
by Aurelio Mistruzzi - 44

R/ CHRISTIANO - POPVLO - RECTOR - ET - PATER - DATVS - VI - NON - MART - A - MCMXXXIX
Pacelli Family coat-of-arms surmounted by tiara and keys

D/ PIVS - XII - PONTIFEX - MAXIMVS - AN - III
Bust of the Pontiff facing left with zucchetto, mozzetta and stole; under the bust: MISTRUZZI

1941 - INVOCATION TO PEACE
by Aurelio Mistruzzi - 44
(Medal, Year III)

R/ MISEREOR - SVPER - TVRBAM
Jesus appears in the centre, surrounded by two mothers and a soldier supporting a wounded companion

D/ PIVS - XII - PONTIFEX - MAXIMVS - ANNO - VI
Bust of the Pontiff facing right with zucchetto, mozzetta and stole; under the bust: MISTRUZZI

1944 - FOR THE SAFETY OF ROME
by Aurelio Mistruzzi - 44
(Medal, Year VI)

R/ DEFENSOR CIVITATIS
An angel carries a cross, holds the heraldic papal coat-of-arms in his left hand; in the background are secular and religious Roman monuments

1950 - HOLY YEAR
by Aurelio Mistruzzi - 44
(Medal, Year XII)

D/ PIVS - XII - ROMANVS - PONTIFEX - MAXIMVS
Bust of the Pontiff facing left with zucchetto and piviale; beneath the bust: MISTRUZZI

R/ EGO - SVM - OSTIVM - PER - ME - SI - QVIS- INTROIERIT - SALVABITVR
The Holy Door with the monogram of Christ. On the sides of the Door: ANNO - JUBI = LAEI - MCMI

1950 - MARIAN CONGRESS
(Devotional Medal)

D/ CONGRESSVS MARIANVS ET DEFINITIO ASSVMPTIONIS B - V - M - ROMAE 1950
Bust of the Pontiff facing left

R/ Allegory of Our Lady's Assumption

191

LA DOMENICA DEL CORRIERE

Supplemento settimanale illustrato del nuovo CORRIERE DELLA SERA - Abbonamenti: Italia, anno L. 1400, sem. L. 750 - Estero, anno L. 2000, sem. L. 1050

Anno 54 — N. 18   4 Maggio 1952   L. 30.—

Il cardellino del Papa. Tutte le mattine, quando Pio XII si fa la barba col rasoio elettrico, un uccellino ammaestrato lasciato libero nelle stanze si posa sulla sua mano sinistra e gorgheggia lietamente accompagnando il lieve ronzio dell'apparecchio. Appena terminata la rapida "toilette" del Santo Padre, il cardellino se ne vola via soddisfatto.
(Disegno di Walter Molino)

Gretel, the injured canary Pius XII found in his garden and befriended, sits on his finger while he shaves. As soon as the Pope finishes, the bird returns to his cage singing joyfully.

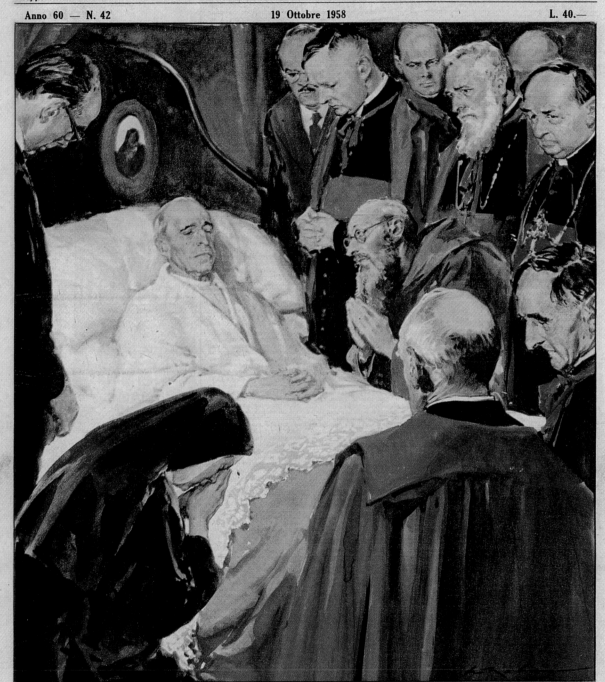

E' morto il Papa. Nel palazzo pontificio di Castelgandolfo, dove si trovava per il solito periodo di riposo, in seguito a un attacco di trombosi, si è spento Pio XII. La fine del Santo Padre, sopraggiunta dopo ansiose alternative di allarmi e di speranze, ha profondamente e dolorosamente impressionato il mondo intero. Nella tavola dedicata al luttuoso avvenimento, il pittore Walter Molino ritrae il morente Pontefice, circondato da alcune delle persone che gli furono vicine nel momento del trapasso. Da sinistra a destra sono: Suor Pasqualina Lehnert, il prof. Gasbarrini, il prof. Galeazzi-Lisi, Mons. Dell'Acqua, Mons. Van Lierde, il card. Tisserant, decano del Sacro Collegio, il card. Canali; inginocchiato padre Clemente, confessore di Sua Santità e, al suo fianco, il card. Pizzardo.

Artist Walter Molino portrays Pope Pius XII who died in Castelgandolfo. Surrounding him are (left to right) Sister Pasqualina Lehnert, Professor Gasbarrini, Professor Galeazzi-Lisi, Monsignor dell'Acqua, Monsignor Van Lierde, Cardinal Tisserant, dean of the Sacred College, Cardinal Canali; kneeling is Father Clemente and, to his side, Cardinal Pizzardo.

199

Pius XII visits the Capranica Seminary.

Wood carving by Arbace Milani.

HOC · IN · CVBICVLO
AB · ANNO · MDCCCLXXXXIV · AD · ANNVM · MDCCCLXXXXV
EVGENIVS · PACELLI
CAPRANICENSIS · COLLEGII · ALVMNVS
COMMORANS
STVDIOSAE · ILLIVS · VIRTVTIS · SPECIMEN · DEDIT
QVA · POSTEA
AD · SVMMI · PONTIFICATVS · APICEM · EVECTVS
VNIVERSAE · ECCLESIAE · PRAEFVLSIT
(A · BACCI)

Roma 26 Settembre 2000

(1)

Io Sr Domenica Mitaritonne dichiaro, anche sotto giuramento, che nel periodo della guerra 1942-1943, ero in via Caboto n°16 Roma. Ho assistito all'ingresso di due o tre famiglie ebree ospitate nelle nostre case con immensa disponibilità da parte delle Superiore, avendo avuto del Vaticano, la sollecitazione di ospitare questi cari fratelli, nelle nostre case. Facevamo a gara col sorriso e l'accoglienza di rendere meno anguste le giornate che trascorrevano nel nostro teatrino. Io e un'altra suore, ci prestavamo tutte le notti, con il freddo o il caldo, a vegliare in finestra per paura dell'arrivo dei tedeschi e, in quel caso, farli nascondere nelle botole del palcoscenico. In una di queste notti, si fermò un camion di Tedeschi sotto le nostre scuole e fu il calzolaio che abitava di fronte, che era malato, ed era in finestra, che disse ai Tedeschi che quello stabile era una scuola elementare. La nostra paura fu enorme, demmo l'allarme agli ebrei di nascondersi. Con fraterno affetto
Sr Domenica Mitaritonne

Letter written under oath by Sister Domenica Mitaritonna stating that orders to offer the Jews hospitality came from the Vatican.

כל המקיים נפש אחת... כאלו קיים עולם מלא

chiunque salva una vita...
è come se avesse salvato il mondo intiero
(Sanhedrin IV. 5)

La Comunità Ebraica di Roma

a **Maestre Pie Filippini**
Via Caboto - Roma

ricordando quanti
a rischio della propria vita
si prodigarono per salvare gli ebrei
dall'atrocità nazifascista

Official recognition from the Jewish Community to the Religious Teachers Filippini "recalling how they risked their lives to save the Jews from nazi-fascist atrocities."

Pius XII with Prince Fahad al Salim from Kuwait, June 15, 1955.

Pius XII with Secretary of State, John Foster Dulles, October 24, 1955.

Pius XII with Pandit Nehru and his daughter Indira Gandhi, July 8, 1955.

Pius XII with President Truman and Mrs. Truman, May 1956.

WARTIME CORRESPONDENCE

BETWEEN

PRESIDENT ROOSEVELT

AND

POPE PIUS XII

PREFACE
BY

HIS HOLINESS POPE PIUS XII

The late Honorable Franklin D. Roosevelt, President of the United States, in his letter addressed to Us on the 14th of February 1940 clearly set forth the purpose he had in mind in sending his Personal Representative to the Holy See. It was that the one so designated by him would be "the channel of communication for any views You and I might wish to exchange in the interest of concord among the peoples of the world."

The correspondence published herewith and the observations and references to be found therein, brief though they be at times and occasioned by circumstances, show how well the appointment has served the purpose intended. Its full significance however was much more far-reaching than this, as may be gathered from a perusal of the letters themselves.

The fortunate outcome of numberless occurrences which arose both during the course of the war and in the post-war period, the solution of urgent problems, the interchange of important information, the organization of American relief which flowed in such generous streams to alleviate the misery begotten of the war, all these would have been well nigh unthinkable and almost impossible, were it not for the designation of a Personal Representative of the President and the magnanimous cooperation and achievements of His Excellency, Mr. Myron Taylor.

PIUS PP. XII

FROM THE VATICAN, *August 6, 1946*

INDEX